W9-BCT-718

Winning Badminton Singles

Winning Badminton Singles

JAKE DOWNEY

Photographs by Louis Ross

EP PUBLISHING LIMITED

First published in 1982 by EP Publishing Ltd,
East Ardsley, Wakefield, West Yorkshire
Copyright © 1982 Jake Downey

This book is copyright under the Berne Convention. All rights are reserved.
Apart from any fair dealing for the purposes of private study, research, criticism
or review, as permitted under the Copyright Act, 1956, no part of this
publication may be reproduced, stored in a retrieval system, or transmitted in
any other form or by any means, electronic, electrical, chemical, mechanical,
optical, photocopying, recording or otherwise, without the prior permission of
the copyright owner. Enquiries should be addressed to the publishers.

Designed by Douglas Martin Associates
Set in 10 on 13pt Plantin
Printed by Robert Hartnoll
Bodmin, Cornwall

British Library Cataloguing in Publication Data

Downey, Jake
   Winning badminton singles.
   1.   Badminton (Game)
   I.   Title
   796.34'5   GV1007

ISBN 0-7158-0823-0 (cased)
      0-7158-0838-9 (limp)

Contents

To the enquiring sportsperson

Badminton is a game and games are a part of sport. The point of the game is to win. However, man created sport for his enjoyment and to enrich the quality of his life. It is fundamental, therefore, that it matters how we participate in sporting activities. In this respect the means matter more than the end. Thus the means of winning in badminton should not lessen the value of the game as a sport.

Preface

Since 1963 my involvement with badminton has been mainly as a teacher and a coach. During that time I have been fortunate to have experienced teaching the game to young players in schools and youth centres and to have seen the same players progress from beginners to a good standard of play at club and county level. In recent years my work has been mainly with international players. The experience of working with the same player for a number of years, whether that player is a youngster in school or a world class competitor, is invaluable for any coach, for it takes time to experiment in the game and try out new ideas in practice.

Not surprisingly, as you learn more about the game you acquire more knowledge to transmit to the players. It is always a problem to decide how to start and progress, and what to include or leave out. Consequently, much time is spent on preparation in an attempt to strip the game down to its bare essentials and then put them into some sort of meaningful order. When this has been done it becomes possible to show how the different parts of the game are connected and to explain clearly why a player should do one thing rather than another. In brief, it becomes possible to theorise about the game. Since the true test of any theory is to try it out in the actual situation one moves constantly to and fro between theory and practice. Practice entails a pragmatic approach to theory: if it works, use it.

I doubt if anyone ever reaches a position in badminton where they can stop and decide that there is nothing more to be said about the theory of the game. It is a dynamic game and change is built into it. There will always be new ideas and theories which develop out of the practical situation. However, it is possible to establish a framework in which theory and practice can develop together. The framework outlined in this book provides a basis for such development. Furthermore, it has been well tested and works successfully in the practical situation.

This book is primarily a practical book; detailed explanations are provided to help any player to improve his performance in the game. It is divided into three parts to make it easier to follow. Because it describes a new approach to badminton, it is important to read the book right through before using it as a reference work to be consulted when advice and information on specific problems are required.

I should like to acknowledge my debt to the many players who have helped me to develop my ideas in the practical situation. The players in the national squads I have worked with since 1970 have co-operated willingly in my experiments on various aspects of the game, both in practice and competition. My especial thanks go to several players who worked closely with me for a number of years during this period – Margaret Lockwood, Gillian Gilks, Paul Whetnall, Ray Stevens and Andy Goode. For a player to work with a coach who continually experiments with new ideas and new ways to improve performance is very demanding and risky for the player. It requires a love of, and genuine interest in, the game; in this situation critical thinking and comments from the players in the evaluation of ideas in practice and competition are vital. Often the value of an idea is not immediately apparent and the player must possess confidence and determination to persevere. These qualities in the players I have worked with have made this book possible. The players were the testers of the theory underlying their practice. And fortunately, in practice all were very successful.

My particular thanks go to Paul Whetnall, who has continually helped me to develop new ideas and try them out and modify them on the practice court prior to completion. In addition, his comments and constant encouragement to complete the work have finally led to the publication of this book.

Jack Downey

Introduction

Imagine the singles player in action. The athlete leaping backwards through space to twist and smash the shuttle away from the opponent. Then landing, sinking lightly, before explosively powering forwards to cover the reply. The kill from the net as he leaps, lunging high, to swoop down on the 'bird' and lash it to the ground. Or, with smooth backward flowing steps, pausing to threaten, holding the opponent still before hitting the gentle dropshot. Now hanging back, inviting the net reply, then gliding into the forecourt to tumble the shuttle tightly over the net.

This is Man not machine, with more to his movement than mere action. There is the underlying purpose. For the body, athletically trained to the highest pitch, serves only to give expression to thought. The movement, so necessary to hit the shuttle, climaxes with strokes used as tactical moves designed to outwit the opponent and gain victory. Through the action we gauge the measure of intelligence, imagination and creative ability. With insight into the tactics of the game we look beyond the action and enjoy the contest between two intelligences, the battle of minds. Though never forgetting nor failing to appreciate the athleticism and the beauty of the movement, we move on to a deeper level of understanding and appreciation.

There is more, for the battle is decided over the duration of time, and thought and skill are only part of the struggle. Can the effort be sustained and fought through with quality until the end result, success or failure, is realised? Can thought be focused singlemindedly on the task in hand, persevering with purpose regardless of the struggle's ebb and flow? Is it possible to ignore the pain of tired body, dismiss the doubts raised by the relentless probing of weaknesses and the negation of strengths, in order to seize opportunities and create victory? Thus we become absorbed with the human element and live with the player, his doubts and fears, his excitement and endeavour. In him Man becomes exposed. The harder the struggle the more we see Man as he is. The expression of his attitude gives colour to his character. Is this the adventurous spirit roaming free to seize its chance or is it tentative caution? Do we see fierce determination, concentration and strength of will glowing forth in the quest, or subdued spirit which succumbs

*to human frailty? Whatever it is we identify with the players, and recognising
what we see in them, we experience ourselves through them.*

*Above all, we acknowledge the arena in which the battle has its setting. We
realise (although we may forget at times) that it is but a game; the rule that
governs all games within the world of Sport applies equally here. That is, all such
contests should be conducted in a fair and sporting manner. It is this feature that
adds the one element of control so necessary to make the occasion an enjoyable one
and thus enriches the total experience for the player and us.*

This description illustrates the different aspects of the game with which
you will be familiar. The intention of this book is to delve deeper into these
different aspects and to give you more insight into the game, and thus to
show you, beginner or world champion, how to become a better singles
player. By knowing the game you will get some idea of what counts as a
'good' player, which is the standard you must aim for. Obviously such a
player must play the game well before you would call him 'good'. So, know
the game and what counts as 'good' and you will be able to take the steps
necessary to become a better player.

What makes a 'good' player is always a favourite topic for discussion.
Various suggestions are put forward and supported by referring to the
attributes of great players from the past. I have read about Dr Dave Freeman
who made few errors, if any, playing with absolute control and accuracy. I
have watched Wong Peng Soon with his impeccable backhand and masterly
courtcraft; Eddy Choong with his speed, agility and dynamic leaps to smash
from all parts of the court; Erland Kops, who personified strength and
power; and I have admired the speed, finesse, artistry and character of Rudi
Hartono.

The Ladies game has had its share of 'good' players, too. I believe the
greatest of these was Judy Hashman (Devlin), who showed marvellous
control and accuracy, great determination, concentration and a fine
understanding of badminton. During the 1970s, Yuki, Lena Koppen,
Gillian Gilks and Margaret Lockwood ruled the Ladies game. Yuki showed
imaginative tactics and positional play; Koppen, supreme fitness and speed
about the court accompanied by superb tactics and a joy of playing; Gilks, a
sound technique and a powerful and dominating overhead game; Lockwood
played with marvellous fluent speed and agility to hit shots with great
control and accuracy.

A summary of these comments would show that opinions about great
players, as examples of what makes a 'good' player, include references to
every aspect of the game. A combination of these features would appear to
be necessary; indeed it is doubtful, as will become apparent later, whether
any one of these attributes is sufficient on its own. So when you read or hear

that a particular player was 'good' because he possessed a big smash, superb fitness, or had character, do not assume that such a feature was the sole reason for that player's success. It is most unlikely that any player, without exception, can become a 'good' player without reaching a high standard in all the various aspects of the game. This book will demonstrate how the different aspects of the game are related and connected into a cohesive whole to form the game that you intend to play successfully.

Part One

The Game

Chapter 1 The Structure of the Game

Tactics and the principle of attack

It is safe to assume that we all know the different aspects of the game to some extent. This is apparent when we talk or read about it. We know that the game includes the skills: the strokes, general movement and footwork. It includes tactics which we know are somehow connected with the skills. Fitness is also related to the skills, and we also realise that certain attitudes play a large part in our performance in the game. We admire the player who can concentrate and show determination in his efforts to win. We experience feelings of fear, frustration, annoyance, joy and excitement which may or may not help us to play better. Finally most of us have a sense of what is correct behaviour in a game with another person. We think fairness is a good thing, as we know because we often talk about such things when we talk about the game and its players.

It is vital for all players and spectators to recognise and understand the connection between the strokes and tactics. This area is central to the game. If understood, then players should play more intelligently and with more imagination to create opportunities to win the contest. Likewise, spectators should appreciate, to a greater extent, the subtleties of the play and the battle of wits between the two contestants.

This is not to exclude the other aspects as unimportant. Indeed they are important. For if a player's attitude is not appropriate and his fitness is not up to the demands of the game then his strokes and tactical play can be affected. The wrong attitude, annoyance, fear, inattention, can divert thought away from the opponent and the best means to beat him. Poor fitness can result in a tired body and affect the stokes and movement about the court, preventing the player from using his strokes effectively as tactical moves to defeat the opponent. If a player cannot reach the shuttle or hit it accurately with control because he is tired, then for all his skill and intelligence he will not possess the necessary instrument – a fit body – to carry out his plans. Tactics are the most important part of the game, for they give meaning to it. Yet they are not part of the game in the same way as strokes and movement, fitness and the attitudes of the player. Tactics cannot be seen physically; they are the underlying ideas which make sense of everything else that the player does on the court during a game. They determine the extent to which all the other parts are used and related to each other. Although, without knowing tactics, it is possible to enjoy the way a player hits the shuttle, his athleticism and grace of movement, and to admire his competitive and sporting behaviour throughout the contest, it is not possible to know what he is trying to do or to appreciate the sense of what he does. It is also impossible to judge what he does as right or wrong, good or bad, appropriate or inappropriate in relation to his opponent and his aim of trying to win the contest.

When a player hits the shuttle to the rearcourt and then travels into position to cover a particular reply, he is applying tactics. Each time he hits the shuttle he should be making a move to obtain a reply which will enable him to make another move or end the rally. Tactics reflect his thinking and also provide the immediate explanation for what he does in a given situation. Yet this is not the full story. We still want to know what makes any choice of tactic appropriate. Why choose one set of tactics and not another? Is it possible to plan tactics? Must we wait until the contest is over before we can decide if the player has acted intelligently? Can we enjoy the tactical skill during the contest? It seems that we can, for many spectators do so. Perhaps this is because players tend to repeat certain patterns of tactical moves during the contest. There is obviously some reason for this which would imply that there is something beyond tactics; some further explanation which provides the underlying rationale and justification for the use of any tactic in the game. What could this be?

The answer is not too difficult to work out. We know the game is a contest and the way to win the contest is to score more points than your opponent. To score a point the shuttle must be hit to the ground or your opponent must make an error. The game is a 'hitting' game in which one player delivers 'blows' to his opponent. The most effective hit is a 'scoring blow'. All the tactical moves are made towards this end. The player should apply the following principle: *At all times try to create a situation in which it is possible to make a scoring 'blow'*. This is the *principle of attack*. It is the most important principle in the development of badminton as an attacking game. It provides the general strategy, that is, the rationale for the use of any tactic.

If tactics are the moves in the game, then strokes are the means of making the moves. If the player applies the principle of attack in the game then the strokes cease to be strokes only and become *stroke-moves*. They become inseparable. This is why the connection between the strokes and tactics is so important. Tactics do no exist without the strokes and the strokes are meaningless in the context of the game unless they carry out the tactics. The other components of the game, fitness and attitude, become important solely because they are necessary to ensure that the player can maintain his chosen tactics throughout the duration of the contest. If the player is lacking in physical strength or firmness of character, then he might be forced to change his tactics during the game. It is not difficult to see how basic fitness and attitude can affect the choice of tactics. For example, you could not choose tactics designed to speed up the game or run your opponent into the ground if your fitness was lacking in strength and endurance, and your attitude lacked adventurousness and patience. The choice of tactics depends on your skill to make the moves and your fitness and attitude to maintain them. You must therefore be capable of carrying out the tactics which you adopt in accordance with the *principle of attack*.

Making a framework for the stroke-moves

The next step is to take all these related parts and connect them up into a meaningful form. This should enable you to gain a deeper insight into the relationship between the parts and get a clearer picture of the whole game. As well as helping you to become a better player this gives you the added advantage of increasing your enjoyment as a spectator.

We can compare this step with building a house. If you take the components of a house – foundations, floor, walls, ceilings, roof, doors, windows, lighting, plumbing, drainage systems – you must then place them in a meaningful order to construct the basic framework for the house. How it looks to us depends on the particular arrangement of the parts into the house. If the parts were arranged differently we would see a different framework. Similarly, how we arrange the parts of badminton will determine the type of framework that we construct and affect how we 'see' the game. It is most important that the framework we construct enables us to see the game in a meaningful way. Whether or not our framework is of value in this respect depends on the use we can make of it. It must, at the least, enable you to answer any queries you may have about the game. For example, it should do the following things:

- give you more insight into the game
- indicate clearly all the moves possible in the game
- enable you to assess what you have or lack in any aspect of the game
- enable you to explain and justify the strategy and tactics adopted by you or your opponent

The immediate problem is how to construct a framework which works. Perhaps some rough guidelines might be formulated by considering how players perform in badminton at the present time. It is quite obvious that to play badminton is not difficult. This is one reason why many people take up the game and derive so much pleasure from it. There is also the possibility of becoming a better player by developing more skill and fitness and gaining further experience in competition. In general, players make steady progress along these lines and, with continual practice and regular play against good opposition, gain further knowledge of the game. Most players, though, just play the game and give little conscious thought to how they do it. In a way this is to be expected for, initially, everyone plays for the enjoyment of hitting the shuttles and moving around the court. Competition, exercise and fun are all that most players want from the game, and in these respects the game has much to offer. As you play and improve, and gain some success, so your enjoyment increases. Why, therefore, should you spend more time making a critical study of the game and perhaps lose some of the enjoyment? There is undoubtedly much common sense in this viewpoint, but it is short-sighted if you want to make further progress as a player or to increase your enjoyment as a spectator. The more you advance in the game the more complex it becomes. You have only to visit a club session, a county match or a tournament, and listen to people talking about the game to realise this. Then (fortunately, if we are to construct a framework) it is quite usual to hear critical discussion take place about all aspects of the game; the strokes and footwork, fitness, behaviour and, above all, the tactics used.

In such discussions judgements are made about some player's performance and reasons offered for what he should or should not have done. It is not unusual after such discussion and argument for many differences to be left unresolved. It is accepted that those involved in debate will argue from different points of view and do 'see' the game differently. You must have experienced this sort of debate, which often ends up in complete disagreement, confusion or agreement to differ. This is where the framework could be so useful. A basic common framework, in which all players talked within the same terms of reference, would eliminate much confusion but still allow for individual interpretation. It would seem, in fact, that almost everyone already operates in a framework of some sort: it is just that they appear to be so different. For example, take a typical framework based on traditional strokes and conventional 'tactics'. A player here might follow the rule to 'hit clears and drops to the corners', as so many young players are advised, in the name of 'tactics'. But as they then slavishly follow that rule no matter who their opponent is, it would hardly appear to be a tactic; for tactics, at the very least, must have something to do with using the strokes as moves to defeat the opponent. The moves must vary with different opponents. Such a player or his advisor will 'see' the game within a very primitive framework in which the connection between strokes and tactics is vague if non-existent. This is not the sort of framework we want to construct. Fortunately, the majority of players do play, though not always consciously, with some connection between strokes and tactics. It is possible to get away with such limited knowledge at the lower levels of play (see page 69), but it is certainly not adequate at the higher levels – although that is not the only reason for learning more about the game. At the lower levels of play too the game can become more interesting and enjoyable the more you know about it.

At the higher levels of play the game becomes more complex and demanding. At this point many players may fail to make further progress.

Such players may possess excellent technical skills and be extremely fit and athletic, but unfortunately do not seem to make intelligent use of these qualities to defeat the opponent. It would appear that they do not know how to go about winning. It is not surprising therefore that many young players, in spite of their obvious talents, tend to suffer defeat at the hands of a thoughtful player. In complete contrast to this, there is the player who is tactically sound and knows what ought to be done to win but meets defeat because he lacks the technical skill and fitness to apply his tactics. Those players who want to take the right steps to win must learn to operate in a clear, well-organised framework, in which the parts are logically connected to form a unified whole.

It seems that we cannot learn much from a study of what players do concerning the construction of such a framework; yet, common to all players, are the basic features inherent in the game. There are the rules, the design and shape of the court, the height of the net, the equipment used (racket and shuttlecock) and the fact that the game is played by humans who move and behave in certain ways. These factors govern all the action and determine the type of action that takes place. It is the game itself which provides the guidelines from which to construct the framework. It is the players who provide us with the starting point. The action of the players should be related to the making of moves to win the contest. It is at that point that we can begin to construct the framework.

Stage 1. The moves in the game

Let us assume that you are learning to operate as a player inside a framework. On this basis we can begin immediately in the game. Each time that you hit the shuttle you make a move which alters your present situation and creates a new one for you and your opponent. The new situation that you create will be either to your or your opponent's advantage, or to the advantage of neither of you; a sort of *status quo* situation. During each rally many different situations will occur as you both create new ones. If we study the situations we can obtain certain information.

In each situation a number of moves are logically possible. For example, imagine that the shuttle is high in your forehand rearcourt. From there you could hit it in various directions with more or less force, to different places in your opponent's court (see figs. 1 and 2). Though certain moves are logically possible not all of them would be appropriate in the situation. For example, it would be silly to play a high floating dropshot from the rearcourt with your opponent waiting ready in the forecourt. A sensible move would be to clear it over his head to the rearcourt – that is, if you are able to hit a shuttle to the rearcourt. If you are a beginner and have to hit the clear from your weaker backhand side, this might prove to be difficult. The suitability of a certain move in a certain situation depends on your ability to perform various strokes. You need technical skill to be able to execute the full range of stroke-moves in any situation. If that skill is lacking then the number of moves you

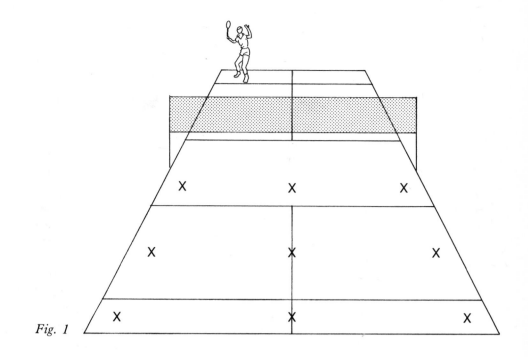

Fig. 1

can make will be limited and that might prove to be of advantage to your opponent (unless, of course, he isn't much of a thinker and doesn't realise your limitations; or, if he does, is too limited himself to exploit them). If you are limited in this way, now is the time to realise it and begin to do something about it. At the least, the framework will draw your attention to all the possible moves that you can learn, so as to be able to select from them in a given situation. What to select takes us to the next stage in the construction of the framework.

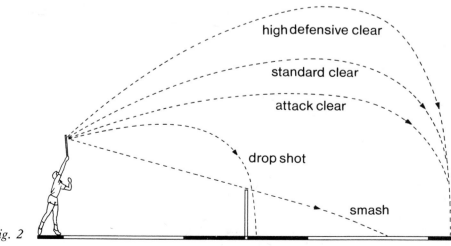

Fig. 2

Stage 2. The principle of attack

How do you know whether or not a stroke-move *is* appropriate? Certainly not until you have made the move and the new situation has been created. Nevertheless you could decide that a move *might* be appropriate. To decide this you must make use of the *principle of attack* (see page 17), which states: 'At all times try to create a situation in which it is possible to make a scoring "blow".' You must make a quick assessment of the present situation, knowing, of course, what is possible. You already know what you can do, so that doesn't require any thought. But you also have to work out what your opponent might do, so you should have a good idea of his capabilities, and what sort of reply might be appropriate from him in that situation. Then, having made a rapid intuitive decision on the basis of your knowledge and understanding of the game and your opponent, you make a stroke-move in accordance with the principle of attack. After the move you still apply the principle of attack and travel to a new position to cover the possible reply in the new situation you have created. Hence you are always thinking ahead and looking for ways to attack the opponent and win the game.

Let us pause for a moment and reflect about this principle of attack. Not only can it provide the rationale for any stroke-move; it can also function as a connecting link for all the moves you make. It cannot really be any other way, for each move that you make should be connected to the next move as part of a pattern designed to create a situation in which you can make a scoring hit. To do this is to base all your moves on the principle of attack. Here is the difference between using your strokes as tactical moves and simply as strokes without any particular purpose.

The idea of the principle of attack acting as a guide in the choice of moves is quite simple to grasp. Next we need to sort out the situations which occur in the game; then we shall be able to work out all the moves that are possible in the game.

Stage 3. The situations

The situations have to be identified, isolated, and then classified. They can be identified quite easily. Fig. 3 shows how the court is divided into three

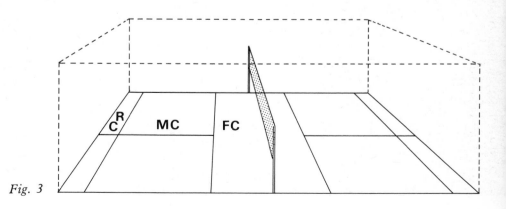

Fig. 3

main areas: the rearcourt (RC), midcourt (MC) and the forecourt (FC). These areas provide the location for all the situations which occur in the game. As the court is rectangular and divided by a net 5ft (1.5m) high it is possible to establish a specific number of situations in each area. This is done by taking the position of the shuttle in the court relative to the height of the net and the player about to hit it. The shuttle is either high or low in the court. In a high position the shuttle is above net height and can be hit in a downward direction. In a low position the shuttle is below net height and must be hit in an upward direction. These positions will vary from very low (near the ground) to very high (the highest point the player can reach to hit the shuttle.) Midway between these two positions, at approximately net height, the shuttle can be hit on a horizontal pathway (see fig. 4). The basic situations are:

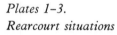

Fig. 4

Plates 1–3.
Rearcourt situations

Rearcourt situations: The stroke-moves are made from high or low positions at the sides and the centre of the rearcourt (see plates 1–3).

Midcourt situations: The stroke-moves are made from high or low positions at the sides and centre of the midcourt.

Forecourt situations: The stroke-moves are made from the sides and the centre. The shuttle position will be clearly above net height, just below or above the top of the net, and near the ground (see plates 4–6).

With these in mind, we can now work out what moves are logically possible in each situation that can develop in the game. We can construct a framework in which we can look at the game as a whole with the situations as the

Plates 4–6.
Forecourt situations

'foundations'. We are in a position to make clear the complete picture we have of the game. Everything there is to know about the game can be discovered by referring to the framework.

Stage 4. The logical structure of the game

We have now reached the final stage prior to constructing the complete framework. What we have done so far is to examine the logical structure of the game by considering all the various parts and the ways they are related to each other, thus ensuring that we obtain the correct components for the framework. The logical structure of the game is summarised in the diagram below.

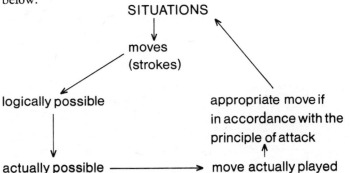

The *framework* is the sum total of all the parts of the game. It is determined by the nature of the game: the court shape and space, the net height, equipment used, rules, and the human limitations of the players.

The *situations* that can occur are determined by reference to the nature of the game and by the position of the shuttle in the court.

The *moves logically possible* are determined by reference to the type of situation from which they are played.

The *moves appropriate* are decided by reference to the principle of attack and a consideration of the position and the ability of the opponent.

The *moves actually possible* depend solely on your ability as a player.

The *move actually played* in a situation will only be appropriate if you make the right decision – that is, if you judge the situation correctly on the basis of the facts you know about your opponent, and then make the move in accordance with the principle of attack to create a new situation which increases your chances of eventually making a scoring hit. If you judge the situation wrongly then it is more than likely that you will make an inappropriate move, one not in accordance with the principle of attack. If you do so you will probably create a situation which is to your opponent's advantage and consequently have to work very hard to regain the advantage. Of course, the ebb and flow as control swings from player to player during the game is part of its fascination for the spectator.

Now we have some guidelines which give us some definite ideas about what the framework should contain and the form it should take, we can begin to construct it.

Chapter 2 The Framework

Plate 7 (left) and 8 (right).
Hits to the rearcourt

In the following pages, the framework is presented in chart form, and is divided into three main sections: rearcourt, midcourt and forecourt situations. All the stroke-moves in each situation are shown and explained in the three charts. When studying the charts, read across the columns from left to right, beginning from the *shuttle position* which determines the type of situation you are in.

When you look at the chart you will notice that all the stroke-moves can be reduced to three basic moves. These are:

1. The hit to the rearcourt – over the opponent's head (see plate 7)
                               – past him at the sides (see plate 8)

2. The hit to the forecourt (see plate 9)
3. The hit to the midcourt – downwards (see plate 10)
                             – horizontally

All the stroke-moves are variations on these three basic moves; they are the different ways in which the moves can be performed. The reasons for these moves are clear. When you hit the shuttle to the rearcourt you force your opponent out of position, away from his central position, and create space; as he goes further away from the net it becomes more difficult for him to make a scoring hit. Your stroke-move to the forecourt also forces him out of

Plate 9.

Hit to the forecourt

position and creates space. A shuttle below net height makes him lift the shuttle and so presents you with a better chance of making a scoring hit. Finally, a downward or horizontal hit to the sides or centre of the midcourt either hits the ground or forces your opponent to lift, which again increases your chances of making a scoring hit. All the strokes are played as moves with this target in mind. To play in this way is to play in accordance with the principle of attack. When we have studied the charts we can refer back to them whenever necessary, to discuss the various moves that can be played in the different situations that occur in the game.

Plate 10.
Hit to the midcourt

Rearcourt Situations

SHUTTLE POSITION	ATTITUDE	INTENTION	STROKE-MOVES	DIRECTION
1. High (at the sides or centre)	**Threatening to attack** (take up the smash position)	1. To cause the opponent to adopt a defensive stance in MC 2. To deceive the opponent	1. Power smash to MC or RC	To centre or sides
			2. Fast sliced smash to MC	Straight or x-court to sides
			3. Fast drop to FC (hit flat or sliced)	To centre or sides
			4. Check-smash to FC	To centre or sides (usually to backhand side)
			5. Attack clear to RC	To sides or centre
			6. Standard clear	To sides or centre
2. High (at sides or centre and to the rear of player)	**Threatening to attack** (jumping backwards into the smash position)	To force opponent to adopt a defensive stance and deceive opponent. To give him less recovery time.	1. Backward jump smash—attack clear—check-smash —standard clear	To sides or centre
3. High (at sides or centre and to the rear of player)	**Defensive** (caught out, off balance and fighting to regain control, in haste)	To get out of trouble and into a stable position. To restore the situation to a neutral one. To make time.	1. Very high defensive clear to RC	To centre
4. Low (on forehand side and to the rear of player)	**Defensive** (set to make a move which will gain the attack)	1. To neutralise the opponent's advantage 2. To deceive	Use a deep or half lunge on diagonal to the FH corner whilst facing the net. Then in balance and can hit: 1. Clear to RC	Straight (down the line)
			2. Drive to MC or RC	Straight or x-court
			3. Drop to FC	To sides or centre
5. Low (on backhand side)	As for forehand side	As for forehand side	1. Underarm clear to RC 2. Drive to MC or RC 3. Drop to FC	– – – – – – –

FUNCTION	OPPONENT'S POSSIBLE REPLIES	YOUR RECOVERY
To hit the ground or force a weak lift	1. Block return to the FC sides or centre 2. Clear to the RC 3. Whip shuttle down line or x-court to RC	Get quickly into balance and travel forwards towards a position to cover the possible replies. Face down the 'funnel' (looking at the opponent waiting to see what he intends to do). This is a slow approach, hanging back to cover the RC and so inviting the reply to the FC, then ready to sprint forwards to attack if the opponent plays a reply to the FC.
To hit the ground or force a weak lift		
To force a lift	1. Net returns to FC 2. Lob to lift over head of 'smasher' to RC	
To cause opponent to scramble from MC defensive stance and may force a weak lift. Played to the backhand side it allows you to cover the 'funnel' and use the forehand smash if the shuttle is lifted. Also used to create space.		
To catch opponent off balance and force a weak reply. To the centre cuts down the angle of reply and make it easier to cover the reply	1. Smash to MC 2. Drop to FC 3. Clear to RC	In balance and travel forwards to MC to take up the defensive or attacking stance depending on how effective the attack clear is. If opponent caught out then take up an attacking stance. If opponent anticipates the clear then quickly take up a defensive stance in the MC.
Send opponent to RC to create space and test him out, keep him moving to discover what he does		Travel to MC and take up a defensive stance
To hit floor in MC or to catch him out of position and cause a weak reply	All the basic replies to these stroke-moves (see above)	Land and recover very quickly to get into balance and sprint towards the MC ready to cover the replies
To drop the shuttle vertically in centre of RC and so make it difficult to time his hit and narrow the possible angle of his replies	1. Smash to the MC or RC 2. Drop to FC 3. Clear to RC	*Walk* calmly back to the MC and take up a defensive stance ready to receive the smash. Alert and watching the opponent to anticipate the reply.
Send opponent to backhand RC	He will be waiting in the MC attacking stance ready to travel to hit the shuttles which are high or low in the RC or MC or FC. He can smash to MC—drop to FC—clear to RC—whip x-court.	Stay in balance whilst hitting the shuttle and then travel forwards to approach the centre whilst facing the opponent down the 'funnel'
Neutralise situation or catch opponent out of position with x-court drive		
To force a lift		

– As for the forehand stroke-moves, though the situation on the backhand side is weaker for most players.– – – – – – – – –
To make a stroke-move from this position is technically difficult and can create a situation with the opponent ready to attack from his stronger forehand side.

Midcourt Situations

SHUTTLE POSITION	ATTITUDE	INTENTION	STROKE-MOVES	DIRECTION
1. High (at sides and centre)	**Threatening to attack** (take up the smash position)	1. To force the opponent to adopt a defensive stance in MC 2. To deceive opponent	1. Power smash to MC or RC	To centre or sides
			2. Sliced smash to MC or RC	To sides
			3. Slash (side arm smash with power or sliced to MC or RC)	To centre or sides
			4. Drop to FC (fast)	To sides
			5. Check-smash to FC	To centre or sides
2. Low (after a fast drop or low reply to the MC)	**Threatening to attack** (alert and racket held ready)	1. To neutralise the situation and create one in which to attack 2. To deceive the opponent	Prepare to hit the shuttle early as you approach it 1. 'Hold and drop' — prepare as if to hit to the RC but then check racket head speed and drop to FC 2. 'Hold and flick' — prepare as if to hit shuttle to FC and then flick the shuttle over opponent's head into RC	To centre or sides
3. Low (after the smash)	**Defensive** (alert fighting attitude)	To get out of the defensive situation and neutralise the advantage of the opponent	1. Block to FC	To centre or sides
			2. Push to MC	To sides
			3. Whip to RC	To sides
			4. Lob to RC	To centre or sides
4. Low (in MC/FC area)	**Attacking** ('fighting attitude')	To prevent the opponent anticipating the stroke-move To deceive the opponent	1. Low serve to FC	To centre or sides
			2. Flick serve to RC	To centre or sides
			3. High serve to RC	To centre or sides
5. Net height	**Attacking** ('fighting attitude')	To counter hit at speed, catch opponent out and force error or weak reply	1. Drive to MC	To sides or centre at opponent
			2. Whip to RC	To sides or centre
			3. Push to MC	To sides or centre
			4. Drop to FC	To sides or centre

FUNCTION	OPPONENT'S POSSIBLE REPLIES	YOUR RECOVERY
To hit a winner or force a weak reply	1. Block to FC 2. Lob to RC 3. Whip to RC	Balanced and in control in the MC. Facing the opponent and ready to attack any reply.
To cause opponent to scramble and make a weak return	1. Low return to FC or MC 2. Clear to RC	
In both moves the opponent is caused to wait or to commit himself before the shuttle is hit 1. To check the opponent and make him pause and so be late for his reply; to make his weight go backwards and then drop the shuttle into the FC	FC attack. Opponent can hit down to MC, drop to FC or lift to RC	Balanced throughout. Alert with racket ready to counter the reply, i.e. to attack or defend.
2. Make his weight come forwards and then flick the shuttle over his head to the RC	1. Smash to MC 2. Clear to RC 3. Drop to FC	
To force the opponent to lift from below the net	Hit down if above net height Lift to FC or RC if below net height	Balanced and alert in an attacking stance, facing the opponent ready for the possible reply in the new situation
To force a lift and prevent him playing a 'spinner' or 'tumbler'	Reply to FC or MC or lift to RC	
To reduce opponent's recovery time and force an error or a mishit	Slash, drop or clear	
To send opponent back to RC	Smash, drop or clear	
To force opponent to lift	Reply to FC or RC	Take up attacking stance
To catch out and force a weak reply	Smash, drop or clear	Take up attacking stance or defensive stance
To send opponent to RC and create space. To make the shuttle drop vertically and difficult for the opponent to time the hit.	Smash, drop or clear	Take up defensive stance
To get shuttle past opponent or force an error or weak reply	Counter drive to MC, whip to RC or drop to FC	Balanced, and maintaining a forward or backward attacking stance according to position of opponent
To force an error or weak reply	Smash, clear or drop	
To cause shuttle to fall quickly and force opponent to hit upwards	Push to MC, drop to FC, lift to RC	
To force a lift	Net reply or lift to RC	

Forecourt Situations

SHUTTLE POSITION	ATTITUDE	INTENTION	STROKE-MOVES	DIRECTION
1. Above net height (travelling upwards from the serve, or a block to the smash or as a low return to the FC or MC)	**Threatening to attack** (take up a forward or backward attacking stance)	To create pressure and force the opponent to take up a defensive stance	1. Slash to MC or RC	Downwards
			2. Brush shot to MC or RC	At or away from opponent
			3. Dab to MC or RC	At or away from opponent
			4. Push to MC or RC	At or away from opponent
			5. Check-smash to FC	Straight
2. Near the top of the net just below net height at sides or centre	**Threatening to attack** (stand in forward attacking stance)	To create pressure and force the opponent to stay in the MC or pause until the stroke-move is made	Tumbler	Straight to FC
			Spinner	Angled towards centre FC
			Tap to FC or RC	Straight
			Whip to RC	Sides
3. Low (near the ground after net reply or drop shot)	**Alert and calm** (fighting attitude)	To take the opponent on in the FC and gain the attack	Hairpin drop	Straight or angled across the net
4. Low (near the ground after a reply to the FC)	**Defensive** (caught out, late to arrive, in haste)	To get out of trouble and into a neutral position. To make time.	High clear	Centre

FUNCTION	OPPONENT'S POSSIBLE REPLIES	YOUR RECOVERY
To hit the ground	'Dig up' the shuttle or 'snatch' it back	Withdraw to edge of FC into attacking stance with racket ready for a weak or unpredictable reply
To hit the opponent or the ground, or to restrict his movements and force a weak reply		
To catch opponent off balance and force a weak reply	FC reply or lift to the RC	
To force opponent to lift or mishit the shuttle	Net reply to FC Clear to RC for both spinner and tumbler	1. Use 'fencer's' movement to withdraw from the net into the forward attacking stance or backward attacking stance depending on how close to the net the shuttle is
To force lift or mishit and reduce the angle of possible replies		
To control a rotating shuttle	Net reply or clear to RC Clear, drop or smash from RC	2. Return quickly to the MC and face the opponent, ready to move forwards or backwards to attack the reply
To get the shuttle past the opponent and force a late or a weak reply	Takes it late and replies with drop to FC, drive to MC or clear to RC	
To 'crawl' over the net and force the opponent to lift or make an error	1. Hit down from above net if poorly executed 2. Reply to FC 3. Clear to RC	Withdraw from the net into the forward attacking stance ready to attack any weak reply
To drop the shuttle vertically in the centre of the RC and make it difficult for the opponent to time his hit. To reduce the opponent's possible angle of return.	1. Smash to MC or RC 2. Drop to FC 3. Clear to RC	Complete the stroke-move, get into balance and walk back to MC to take up a defensive stance. Calm and alert, watching the opponent to anticipate the reply.

Chapter 3 Comments on the Framework

The contents of the charts

The charts contain all the different factors that you must take into account in each situation. The *shuttle position* determines the situation. The *principle of attack* should account for all the other factors.

Attitude and *intention* are closely related. *Intention* refers to your tactic in a situation and this is reflected in your attitude as you set about your task. Generally, attitude is a far more complex factor than I have described it as here. It covers a whole range of psychological states. For the sake of simplicity and clarity I have suggested that, in the context of the game, your tactical attitude should appear to your opponent as if you were getting ready to attack. Your attitude is seen in your behaviour as you purposefully and positively get ready to attack in a situation.

I am suggesting here that you should adopt an attacking attitude, even when you are in a defensive situation. There are numerous words which might be used to describe your behaviour as you get ready to deal with the situation: determined, aggressive, careful, forceful, positive. So far, I have simply described the behaviour I believe is required as 'threatening to attack' or 'adopting a fighting attitude'. Your intention is related to this. For usually, if your opponent believes you are able to attack effectively, he will guard against the strongest threat to him. He is compelled to anticipate only the strongest move against him which is the one that may cause him to make a reply to your advantage.

In making his preparation in anticipation of one move only, your opponent allows you to make other moves which may catch him out and cause him to make a hasty or weak reply. Hence, an additional benefit to be gained from your attitude is that it places pressure on the opponent. Just imagine yourself in his position. There he is, facing a player who always seems to be in a position to attack. There is no let-up for him. All this is achieved before you actually hit the shuttle and make your move. You cannot achieve that effect without a great deal of hard physical work, skilful stroke production and tactical understanding; yet it is what you must achieve if you want to become a better player.

The *stroke-moves* listed are those which are logically possible. Of these moves some are appropriate to the situation and others are not. The appropriateness of a move is determined by the principle of attack. With some study and experience you should quite easily work out all the moves possible and appropriate in a situation. When you play an opponent you should be able to judge what alternative moves are open to you in a certain situation and consequently what sort of situation you will create when making a specific move. If you play intelligently you will avoid creating a situation to your disadvantage.

The *direction* in which the shuttle is hit is also important. For example, you might be in the centre rearcourt ready to smash. You know that your opponent defends with a forehand grip. If you smash to his forehand he can make all the possible replies. Whereas if you smash to his backhand side he can only reply with the straight block to the forecourt. Thus you aim your smash to the backhand side to create a situation to your own advantage.

The *function* of each stroke-move is quite obvious. Whether or not a stroke-move fulfils its function depends on how well you execute it and how well your opponent can reply to it. The *opponent's possible replies* are simply a list of the stroke-moves possible in that situation. The list enables you to check off what your opponent actually can do. If you know what replies he can make in a situation you can then travel to cover these replies. Your *recovery* will be based on what replies your opponent can make. Watch the opponent for clues as to what he may do as you travel into position to cover the possible replies. You will still see the shuttle in your field of vision but your main focus will be on your opponent. Your attention is only on the shuttle when the opponent hits it and you travel into position to make your reply. The opponent remains within your field of vision but, at that point, is of secondary importance.

Try to avoid making any stroke-move where you cannot recover to maintain the attack. Make sure that you can actually cover all the replies. If not you will either lose the rally or find yourself doing a lot of extra work to retrieve the situation. Percentage badminton is based on being able to recover and deal with the opponent's replies to your stroke-moves. Adventurous badminton, where you take a calculated risk with the possibility of failure or not being able to cover the reply, usually occurs in the forecourt where there is more chance of a kill. In such a situation it is unlikely that the opponent can make a reply and if he does it will probably be a weak or lucky one. Thus, if you get to the shuttle, the chances of success are high and the adventurous risk would be justified. In such a situation the rule is 'commit yourself' and go for the winner. Avoid doing so in the rearcourt when you are off balance and consequently too late in recovering to cover the replies. This is more reckless than adventurous.

Rearcourt situations

Situation 1   *Shuttle position.* You travel to the rearcourt and prepare to hit the shuttle from a high position.

Attitude. This is reflected in the physical position you take up to make your stroke-move. If you play in accordance with the principle of attack you will work hard to get into the 'smash position'. Once in that position you can play any attacking stroke-move. For most players the smash position is the most difficult to take up for it requires hard work, speed and strength to do so consistently. It is very important that you do adopt the smash position for it imposes the strongest threat to the opponent (see plate 11).

Plate 11.
Smash position

Intention. Your intention is closely linked to your attitude. Your intention in taking up the smash position is to force the opponent to defend against your strongest threat. Thus he should take up the 'defensive stance' (see plate 12). He cannot anticipate your stroke-move until you hit the shuttle, so

Plate 12.
Defensive stance

you can deceive him. You can play a variety of moves and perhaps catch him out with the attack clear or the check-smash. Deception is simply the art of looking as if you are about to do one thing, so that the other player comes to believe that that is what you intend to do, and then doing something else. The point of deception is to make the opponent prepare for one sort of stroke-move and so prevent him anticipating some other move you might want to make.

Stroke-moves. The column on the chart describes the strokes that you can use as moves in the situation. The first four stroke-moves are seen as moves which maintain the attack. Ideally they all originate from a balanced-smash position. The smash position is itself tactical for even before you hit the shuttle your opponent sees it and takes up a defensive stance. The opponent must know that you can hit a powerful smash for, if not, he will not take up a defensive stance; then your other moves will not be as effective in getting the reply you want. The first four moves, being downward hits, deny your opponent the chance to make a scoring hit. If they are successful, he is forced to lift the shuttle. All place him in a midcourt or forecourt defensive situation.

The fifth move, the 'attack clear', is used as a variation on the smash and is very effective if you have forced him to take an alert defensive stance. It does, however, create a situation where a quick opponent gets the opportunity to gain the attack and hit downwards.

The sixth move is described as the 'standard clear'. This is used simply as a manoeuvring move to send the opponent out of position and into his rearcourt. In the early stages of a match, if you do not know your opponent, it is used to find out what he does in the rearcourt situation. From what he does you get to know his possible replies and you soon learn if he has a powerful smash. If you find that he cannot threaten you, then you can always use this knowledge to make time or manoeuvre him around the court whilst you create some new advantageous situation.

Situation 2   The stroke-move is the 'backward jump smash' (see plate 13). It is used when your opponent whips the shuttle over your head to the rearcourt and you have to jump backwards to make an early reply. Of course from this position you could also clear or drop the shuttle. The smash is used to catch the opponent out with the quickness of your reply. It is vital here that you recover extremely quickly to cover the possible replies, for the hit takes place in the middle of your backward jump and you still have to land and regain balance before recovering to travel forwards to cover the replies sufficiently early to maintain the attack.

Direction. The shuttle must travel forwards but the direction can vary between straight (on a parallel pathway to the sideline) down the side or at the opponent, and angled (on a diagonal direction from one side of the court to the other). Angled directions are also described as cross-court (x-court). The shuttle is hit in a certain direction as a move according to the principle of attack.

Function. It is the function of each stroke-move to alter the present situation and create a new one to your advantage. The move will succeed in this if the stroke is well executed. For example, you might attempt the appropriate move but perform the stroke badly and so the move would fail to function as it was intended. You should make sure that you are technically equipped to make the moves you select to win the rally. Good technique reduces the possibility of making errors in stroke production and increases the possibility of making a successful move. This is one important reason for regular practice.

The opponent's possible replies. If you hit the shuttle downwards your opponent can only hit it upwards from below net height. Although he can vary the height, speed, distance and direction of his replies you will still keep the advantage, for you retain the possibility of hitting downwards. Only if you hit an attacking or a standard clear over your opponent's head do you create a situation which allows your opponent to gain the attack and possibly hit downwards. So be aware of this when you use the clear as a move. If your opponent sees that you are balanced and in a position to smash he will take up a defensive stance and you may catch him out with your attack clear and check-smash. But if he whips the shuttle past you and you have to perform a backward jump smash then he will most probably take up an attacking stance in his midcourt and threaten your move with an early

Plate 13.
Backward jump smash

reply, in which case you could lose the advantage to be gained from a smash. If you clear you must ensure that the shuttle reaches the rearcourt, for if not, you give your opponent the attack and the positions are reversed. Make sure, when attacking from the rearcourt, that you hit the shuttle accurately and with control so that it goes where you intend it to as a tactical move. *Your recovery.* What you do after making a stroke-move is most important. You should travel to a position which enables you to cover the replies to your move. Let us imagine that you have used a power-smash directed down the line to the backhand side of your opponent. He has the choice of the following moves. He can block to the forecourt, lob over your head to the rearcourt, push or whip the shuttle at you or away from you. All these stroke-moves require an upward hit. What should you do? Most players find that the speed of the power-smash usually restricts the reply to a block to the forecourt. But if you begin rushing forwards he may be tempted to flick the shuttle over your head and catch you out. So really you want to 'invite' him to make a reply to the forecourt or midcourt so that you can travel forwards and hit downwards from nearer the net. At the same time you want to avoid creating a situation which allows him to catch you out with a reply to the rearcourt or a whip cross-court away from you. After you have smashed, travel diagonally forwards towards the centre while remaining mainly in the rearcourt. You 'hang back', closing the door on any replies to the rearcourt. It is as if you travel forwards on a slowly moving base whilst facing the opponent down the funnel (see fig. 5) to cover his replies.

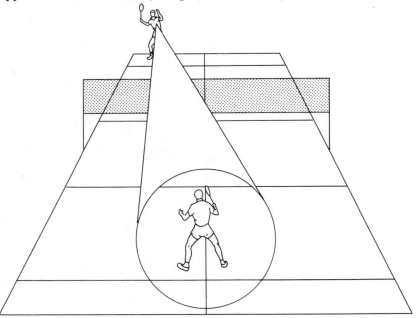

Fig. 5

This policy invites the reply to the forecourt which you can attack. This is where most of the scoring hits are made. Watch to see what your opponent will do and immediately he blocks to the forecourt, you can travel quickly forwards to attack. If he does lift high to the rearcourt then the original situation is recreated and you commence the attack once again. If he whips the shuttle cross-court away from you then you must deal with a rising shuttle travelling quickly away from you. However, if you are facing down the funnel and have remained in the rearcourt you should be in a position to make a downward hit and so maintain the attack (fig. 6).

If you hit the standard clear or attack clear then you would travel forwards and take up a defensive position in the midcourt, square on to the opponent and ready to defend against a downward hit. Of most importance here is that you recover extremely quickly, and perhaps have to sprint towards the midcourt to cover the possible replies.

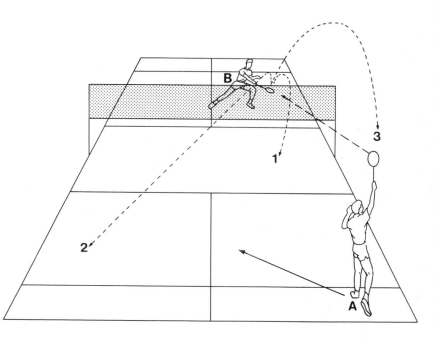

Fig. 6

A smashes and then travels slowly forwards towards the midcourt.
Replies
1.   B blocks to FC. A sprints forward to hit down or play a spinner or tumbler.
2.   B whips cross-court away from A. A sprints across to intercept and hit down.
3.   B lobs to the RC. A steps back into smash position.

The word 'funnel' is used to describe the position of one player relative to another. Usually a player divides the angle of direction of the possible returns of his opponent, i.e. for shots passing on his right and left sides. However, badminton is a three-dimensional game and the shuttle can be hit upwards as well as to the left and the right sides of the player. After making a move the player should try to position himself square on to the opponent even whilst travelling into position. He then appears to be looking down a funnel and, like a goalkeeper, attempts to cover all the possible space to prevent the shuttle getting past him.

Situation 3   Another typical situation occurs when the shuttle is high at the sides or the centre. This time we will assume that the shuttle has been flicked over your head to the rearcourt too quickly for you to get into a position to use the smash as a move. Your opponent has created a situation in which you are off balance and in haste.

Your *attitude* is one of 'active defence', when you are in a defensive situation but make a move used to regain the attack. Your *intention* is solely to get out of trouble and to alter the present situation to one that, if not to your advantage, is more evenly balanced. And for this you need time to recover.

The best *move* in this situation is to hit a very high clear directed to the centre of the opponent's rearcourt (but make sure that it travels the full distance to the rearcourt). The *function* of this move is to reduce the angle of possible returns and to give you time. Then you can literally walk back to the midcourt and take up the defensive stance. In fact you will find the walk is quite therapeutic for it has a calming and steadying effect. Now you are ready, calm and alert to defend against your opponent's replies. The moves actually possible will be determined by what your opponent can do with the shuttle dropping vertically in the centre of the rearcourt. So, although your opponent is the attacker, in adopting active defence you have created a neutral situation which can easily be turned to your advantage. On such an occasion it would help if you had studied your opponent and found out what he was inclined to do in this sort of situation.

Situation 4   The fourth situation has the *shuttle position* low on the forehand side and to your rear. Your *attitude* is one of active defence. You want to get out of trouble and create a situation which will improve your chances of attack. Usually in this situation the opponent is poised in his midcourt ready to hit down any weak replies. Your *intention* is to neutralise your opponent's advantage and if possible to deceive him and so prevent him from anticipating your reply. For that reason you must be in balance when making your stroke-move for it requires a deep or half lunge backwards towards the forehand corner (see plate 14) and the shuttle is taken late as it falls below net height. The moves you can make are limited but still relevant to the principle of attack. These are:

1.   A clear directed down the line to make your opponent travel to the backhand rearcourt away from his central position.
2.   A drive directed straight or x-court to give the opponent less time or to catch him out and force a weak reply.

Plate 14.
Backward forehand lunge

3. A low reply to the forecourt directed straight or angled and used to make time to recover and force the opponent to hit upwards.

You can deceive your opponent and turn this situation to your advantage only if you are in balance and capable of making all these stroke-moves. Thus you force your opponent to wait and see what move you actually make or you can make him commit himself by looking as if to play one move and then playing another. Your *recovery* will depend on the situation you create with your move. The important point is to remember to stay in balance to complete the stroke-move before recovering into position to cover your opponent's possible replies. If you hit the clear to the rearcourt, you should travel quickly forwards and take up a defensive stance in the midcourt. If you play a drive stroke-move you will have less time to recover if your opponent intercepts it, so you should travel quickly to the midcourt and take

Plate 15 (above).
Forward attacking stance
Plate 16 (below).
Backward attacking stance

up an attacking stance. If your dropshot to the forecourt is successful, you can travel forwards to take up a forward or backward 'attacking stance' on the edge of the forecourt ready to threaten any replies into the forecourt (see plates 15 and 16).

Situation 5   This is identical to the previous situation but on the backhand side and thus more difficult for the right-handed player. The pattern is the same as for the forehand side. For most players this is a weak position, for technically many players lack the ability to make all the possible moves in this situation. Any replies are usually played to the opponent's stronger forehand side. Usually this situation does not occur in good standard men's singles and if it does, men normally use a backhand flick clear to get out of trouble. It is seen more frequently in the ladies game when the whip cross-court may get the shuttle past the lady and force her into this situation on the backhand side. Some ladies, particularly in Denmark, have developed a strong underarm clear or sidearm drive from that position which is most effective as a move to get out of trouble and gain the attack. It is a situation which can be created and any player should consider the moves possible in accordance with the principle of attack in that situation. Then it is a matter of developing the technique to make the stroke-moves.

Midcourt situations

Situation 1   The *shuttle position* is high at the sides or centre of the court. Your *attitude* is threatening, ready to attack, and so you take up the smash position. Your *intention* is to force the opponent to adopt a defensive stance. You can then make him wait until you hit the shuttle before he prepares for his reply. At the same time you are more able to deceive him if necessary – though really there is not much need for deception if you are nearer to the net for you should be able to make an effective attacking move without using deception.

The *stroke-moves* are all strong attacking moves, for the shuttle is hit downwards with a smash, slash (sidearm action), fast drop or check-smash. The *direction* is straight or angled across the court or, if hit from the centre, straight at your opponent or angled away from him to the sidelines. The *function* of the moves is to hit an outright winner or to force a weak lift. Your *opponent's possible replies* under this heavy pressure are: the block to the forecourt, lob to the rearcourt, and the whip to the rearcourt, either cross-court, down the sides or straight at you. Your *recovery* should be balanced and controlled, quickly alert in the attacking stance in the midcourt ready to attack any replies. In fact you are in a very strong position in this situation and should ensure that you seize the opportunity to make a scoring hit.

Situation 2   The *shuttle position* is low after a fast drop or a low return to the midcourt. Your *attitude* is again that of attack and so even with the low position of the shuttle you should be alert and determined in your *intention* to neutralise your opponent's advantage. You want to create a situation to enable you to gain the attack. To do this some deception is necessary. Your *stroke-move* is to take the shuttle early and to play a drop into the forecourt or to flick it over the opponent's head or past him down the sides into the rearcourt. The *direction* can be straight or angled. It is because your opponent is ready to attack the shuttle as it rises that you need to use some deception. Thus you should look as if you are going to make a specific move and either cause the opponent to pause or make him commit himself in a particular direction. If you can make him transfer his weight slightly towards one direction then you can catch him out by hitting the shuttle in another direction away from him.

This situation is similar to that experienced by players in many games; soccer, rugby and basketball players often feint to go one way to wrong-foot a defender in order to get past. To do this they use body sway or check their speed and then accelerate away when the opponent has been deceived. In boxing, karate, aikido, judo and fencing the athletes constantly make use of feints (deceptive movements) to outwit the opponent and gain the upper hand in a situation. This deception is a very necessary part of most contest games.

To deceive your opponent in this particular situation you should prepare to hit the shuttle and begin your stroke-move, but delay the hit to force your opponent to wait or make him commit himself to prepare his reply. There are two basic ways of doing this:

1. Prepare as if to hit the shuttle firmly upwards and as your opponent's weight goes backwards, check the action and play a drop into the forecourt.
2. Prepare as if to hit the shuttle into the forecourt but delay actually making the hit. Then as your opponent's weight comes forward, flick the shuttle quickly over his head, or past him into the rearcourt.

The *opponent's possible replies* are to attack the shuttle in the forecourt or to travel quickly to attack from the rearcourt. His success in doing this depends largely on how effective your deception has been. Your *recovery* must be quick and you should be balanced and alert ready to attack the replies from the forecourt or rearcourt.

Situation 3 The shuttle position is low after a strong downward hit from the opponent. Your *attitude* is defensive as reflected in your alert, balanced, defensive stance. Your *intention* should be to neutralise the opponent's attack and to get out of the defensive situation. And in this situation you should realise that the shuttle will be coming towards you at great speed and much control is required. You must keep calm and let the shuttle come to you rather than try to do anything special with it. In the defensive situation take up a fighting attitude, similar to that which you take up when preparing to catch a hard ball thrown at you. The hands are ready to give with the ball as you absorb the force and slow it down. Similarly, in receiving the smash you must present your racket face to the shuttle and keep it in line with the shuttle whilst you make your stroke-move.

When you play the block to the smash as a *stroke-move*, your racket face should meet the shuttle square on, perhaps with some underspin, and the racket head will give slightly to absorb the force, slow the shuttle down and give you control (see plate 17). The *function* of the block is to return the shuttle into the forecourt so that it drops below net height before the opponent can travel to the net to hit your return down to the floor. Thus it is a race to see if you can get the shuttle over the net and below the net height before he reaches it. If you win then he will be forced to hit upwards and you can regain the attack.

Plate 17.
The block

Another *stroke-move* in this situation is to push the shuttle in a low return to the midcourt. The *function* of this is to prevent the opponent making his reply from close to the net and reduce the number of replies open to him. The situation is once again evenly balanced. With practice you can meet the smash early and drive or whip the shuttle horizontally at the opponent, down the line past him or cross-court away from him.

These are all moves intended to force a hasty reply or an error and so enable you to regain control of the situation. A further move is to flick the shuttle upwards over your opponent's head to the rearcourt. This move may wrong-foot the opponent who rushes in after his smash, and cause him to be late in travelling back to the rearcourt, making it difficult for him to attack effectively. In any case it creates space and places him once again in the rearcourt with the problem of creating a situation in which he can make a scoring hit. The *opponent's possible replies* vary according to your stroke-move. To the block reply he can hit down if above net height, or play a spinner or tumbler into the forecourt, or lift it to the rearcourt if it is below net height. Your *recovery* after the block is to take up an attacking stance, threaten his reply to the forecourt and perhaps force him to lift high and give you the attack. From your push to his midcourt, he can drop to the forecourt, whip the shuttle back at you in the midcourt or clear it to the rearcourt. This is where he could use his deception to outwit you. Your *recovery* therefore should be alert and balanced in an attacking stance in the midcourt ready to intercept his reply.

If you drive or whip the shuttle cross-court or down the sides then you must recover quickly in case he intercepts the shuttle and hits it down to your midcourt. Your recovery may take the form of an attacking stance or defensive stance depending on how successful your move has been. Finally, if you clear the shuttle over his head, as a move to the rearcourt, the situation repeats itself and you recover into a defensive stance.

Situation 4   In this situation the *shuttle position* is low for it is the opening move of each rally: it is the 'serve' (see plates 18 and 19). In general, insufficient thought is given to the use of the serve as a move in the game; it is merely believed to be important. Your *attitude* should be one of 'readiness' to attack, shown in your calm and alert serving stance. Your *intention* is to prevent the opponent anticipating the type of serve, with the possibility of deceiving him sufficiently to obtain a weak reply. The *stroke-moves* open to you are: a low serve to the forecourt, a flick serve over the head of your opponent to the rearcourt and a high defensive serve to the rearcourt. The low serve directed to the centre reduces the angle of possible returns. The flick serve and high serve can be directed to the sides or the centre. The *function* of the low serve is to reduce the angle of returns and to force a lift. The flick serve is used as a move to catch out the opponent and force a weak reply. The high defensive serve-move is intended to drop the shuttle vertically into the rearcourt and

Plates 18 and 19.
The serve

make it difficult to hit, and also to send him out of position and create space.
Your *opponent's possible replies* to the low serve are:

1. A drop to the forecourt.
2. To hit down into the midcourt if he is quick enough to attack as it crosses the net.
3. To clear it to the rearcourt.

The high serves offer him three possible moves, the smash to the midcourt, drop to the forecourt and the clear to the rearcourt. Your *recovery* after a low serve is to take up the attacking stance and threaten any replies to the forecourt. After a successful flick serve-move, take up the attacking stance. If your opponent travels quickly and looks as if he can smash the serve then take up a defensive stance. The high serve will obviously be easy to smash and so it is sensible to take up the defensive stance to cover this possible reply.

Forecourt situations

Situation 1 The first situation is shown with the *shuttle position* above net height, having travelled up from a block to the smash, a net return to attacking shots, or from a dropshot from the rearcourt.

Your *attitude* is attack with the *intention* to threaten, create pressure and force your opponent to pause and adopt a defensive stance before he has fully recovered from making his reply. You should try to take the shuttle as early as possible to obtain the maximum effect. To do this you may have to stretch to meet it and this you can do with a lunge or jump lunge (see plate 20). The stroke-moves possible are a slash, brush shot, dab or push and check-smash. The slash is used to hit severely downwards for the outright winner. The others are controlled strokes (to avoid hitting the net) and *directed* at or away from your opponent. The *function* of these three moves will be to get the shuttle past your opponent, to hit the ground or to restrict his movements and force a hasty or weak reply. The function of the check-smash is to catch

Plate 20.
Jump lunge

him out going backwards to defend. Your *recovery* is most important. To make the move you will most probably have been adventurous and fully committed in attacking the shuttle. Now you must withdraw from the net to the edge of the forecourt ready to counter the reply. You should travel back quickly into the attacking stance with your racket ready to hit down any replies.

The *opponent's possible replies* are quite limited if your attack has been successful. The most he can do is to somehow 'dig up' the slash or snatch back the other shots without much control. Now, if you have recovered properly, you should have no difficulty in ending the rally.

Situation 2   The *shuttle position* is near the top of the net but just below net height at the sides or centre of the forecourt.

Your *attitude* is attack with the *intention* to threaten, create pressure and force your opponent to pause and adopt a defensive stance. You can make this happen if you approach the shuttle with your racket head up, ready to hit downwards. Always be optimistic in this way and look as if you could attack the shuttle from above net height. It does create pressure on the opponent to know that you are always ready to threaten and seize the chance to hit downwards. If the shuttle has fallen below net height when you arrive to hit it then it is a simple action to lower the racket head to hit the shuttle from below. The *stroke-moves* used create a situation which will enhance your chances of making a scoring blow. These are:

1.   *The tumbler*. The shuttle is hit with a glancing blow from below with the side or top edge of the racket leading the movement. This causes it to rotate around its horizontal axis into a tumbling action. Hence its name.

2.   *The spinner*. The racket face strikes the shuttle with a glancing blow on the side which causes it to rotate around a vertical axis in a spinning motion. The effect of both of these moves is to keep the shuttle close to the net and make it difficult for the opponent to return the shuttle with control. For this reason both are attacking moves even though hit upwards. To perform them with control requires much care and attention. You should ensure that you complete the move before recovering into a position for the reply. The *direction* of the tumbler is straight across the net. The spinner is hit straight or to the centre.

3.   *The tap*. This is used to make a reply to a tumbler or spinner. The shuttle is simply given a very quick light tap to return it into the forecourt, and a very quick stronger tap to hit it to the rearcourt. The quickness of the 'tap' reduces the time that the racket face is in contact with the rotating shuttle and eliminates the effect of the rotation. It is thus possible to gain some degree of control over the shuttle and make an effective move in the situation. The *direction* is straight.

4.   *The whip*. Used to whip the shuttle from near the top of the net past the opponent to the rearcourt. The direction is straight or cross-court.

The *function* of these stroke-moves varies slightly. The moves to the forecourt are used to force the opponent to mishit or lift the shuttle. The moves to the rearcourt are played at speed to get the shuttle past the opponent and force an error or a weak reply.

The *opponent's replies* to the net moves are to return the shuttle close to the net into the forecourt, to whip it past you if possible, or to lift it up to the rearcourt. If you succeed in getting the shuttle past him to the rearcourt then he will usually have to take it low in the rearcourt. Then he uses the moves possible in that situation.

Your *recovery* varies with the situation that you have created. You should recover from the net-moves by withdrawing slightly from the net to the edge of the forecourt in a forward or backward attacking stance depending on how close to the net the shuttle is. If you have hit the shuttle past the opponent to his rearcourt, withdraw to the midcourt and take up an attacking stance ready to threaten any reply.

Situation 3 The *shuttle position* is low though very close to the net. Your *attitude* is defensive, very alert and prepared to concentrate and take much care in making the move. Your *intention* is to take the opponent on in the forecourt, and try to force him to lift the shuttle. To do this you use a 'hairpin drop' (see plate 21) as a stroke-move. The *function* of this is to hit the shuttle gently so that it 'crawls' up and over the net too close to the net for the opponent to hit it downwards. Thus, if successful, you will force him to lift as he makes a *reply* back to the forecourt or high to the rearcourt. If the move is badly executed you present him with the chance to hit downwards or whip the shuttle past you for a scoring hit. Your *recovery* is to withdraw slightly from the net and take up the 'attacking stance' on the edge of the forecourt.

Plate 21.
Hairpin drop

Situation 4 The shuttle position is very low, usually after the block to the smash. Your *attitude* is defensive for you have been caught out of position and are late to arrive to hit the shuttle. You are in a hurry and having to scramble to get to the shuttle and hit it before it reaches the ground. Your *intention* is to get out of trouble and neutralise the situation and gain time in which to recover. The *stroke-move* used in this situation is the high defensive clear to the centre of the opponent's rearcourt. Its *function* is to make time for you, cause the shuttle to drop vertically in the rearcourt, make it more difficult to time the hit, and also narrow the angle of possible replies. The *possible replies* are the clear to the rearcourt, drop to the forecourt and smash to the midcourt. Thus your *recovery* is to walk calmly back to the midcourt and take up the alert defensive stance whilst watching the opponent to see what he does. This situation is similar to the third rearcourt situation (see p. 44).

The advantages of the framework

The framework provides a list of the situations which occur in the game, for all situations take place in the sections contained in the charts. The shuttle position can be placed within the rearcourt, midcourt or forecourt, in high or low positions. A study of the charts and careful observation of the game will confirm this. Consequently it is possible to list all the situations, and all the known stroke-moves, plus any new ones which develop.

There is much scope for you to use your imagination and express your individuality. Even though certain moves are suggested as appropriate in each situation, in accordance with the principle of attack, there is no specific instruction about when and how these moves are to be made. The choice and execution of a stroke-move would be a matter for you to decide. You are free to devise all kinds of stroke habits and variations which can be used to deceive, outwit and mislead opponents. There is even scope for you to invent an entirely new way of hitting the shuttle as occurred recently when the Malayan players, the Sidek brothers, began to serve low with the feathers pointing downwards causing the shuttle to swerve and dip in its flight. There is even the possibility of developing higher levels of performance within the game when one considers what is logically and humanly possible within such a framework. There is a slight difference even though the two are interdependent. For example, it is logically possible, as a valid stroke-move, to block the opponent's smash in the forecourt and not the midcourt as usually happens in singles play. Not just in the forecourt, but right off the top of the net as a tennis player does when he volleys. But whether that is humanly possible as a move in singles is debatable. It would require a player to develop power, lightning reflexes and brilliant anticipation, for he would have to wait until his opponent was committed to his stroke before travelling forwards to anticipate the smash. An early forward movement would allow his opponent to clear over his head to the rearcourt. I have no doubt that eventually a player could develop the athletic ability, skill and confidence to make such a move but until such time it is doubtful whether it will be seen as a stroke-move in the singles game.

There is no reason why players cannot begin to take the shuttle much earlier in practice though to do so requires attention to the art of moving about the court. This art is vital to performing various strokes as tactical moves. A high level of gymnastic and athletic ability would enable a player to play stroke-moves with effect in creating situations to make scoring hits. Such ability focuses attention on another example of how the game could develop within the framework. It is quite possible, for instance, to take the shuttle much earlier in both the rearcourt and the forecourt when on the attack. A player could leap backwards from the midcourt, smash, land in the rearcourt, recover to step forwards and leap from the midcourt to kill the shuttle in the forecourt. This is possible, simply because the court is only 22ft (6.7m) long on one side of the net, and a leap forwards or backwards from the midcourt need only be of 8–9ft (2.4–2.7m) to reach the shuttle. Such a leap is well within the capabilities of a good athlete. The difficult part is to land lightly and recover quickly, but again this is not difficult in a trained athlete. Such stroke-moves would be in accordance with the principle of attack and would simply speed up the rate at which the moves were played. This would increase the pressure on both players but would place more demands on the opponent who would have to combat such stroke-moves. This sort of development is inevitable within the framework for, with the onset of professionalism, the players are able to devote more time to developing their fitness and athletic skill in moving; and coaches and sport scientists can apply the training methods which develop from the study of skilled movement in other sports. Inevitably, as all players develop their athletic ability to travel quickly around the court to make tactical moves, some of the moves would lose their tactical effect as the opponents would also acquire the ability to make such moves. The end result would be that the moves would still be in accordance with the principle of attack but rallies would be longer and the game played at a faster pace. This would make the game more dynamic and exciting to play and more enjoyable to watch. All such developments depend solely on what is logically and humanly possible, and what is the most effective method of making attacking moves in accordance with the principle of attack. Intelligent use of the framework will prevent your play from becoming stereotyped and predictable, for it will provide you with many opportunities to anticipate and create new developments in the game. It will give you the freedom to be more imaginative and creative. It will release you from fixed ideas and allow you scope for individual interpretation of the tactical problems that arise during the contest.

You can use the 'principle of attack' to make the appropriate stroke-moves during the game. This is not intended to imply that you must try to smash your way through your opponent at every opportunity. It simply means that any stroke-move is played to create a situation which increases the eventual likelihood of hitting a winner. In fact, you can and should apply the principle of attack in a defensive situation. Let me explain. Because you want to attack you should adopt an attacking attitude even when waiting to receive the smash. This is important, for you must learn to concentrate and work hard to play an attacking move in that situation. Your block to the smash should be valued as an attacking move, for it is an attempt to return the shuttle over the net and below net level in the forecourt before your opponent has travelled forwards to hit down your reply. If you get the shuttle below net level before he reaches it then he must hit the shuttle upwards even to make a simple net reply. You are immediately placed in a better situation to make a scoring hit.

From the same defensive situation, the flick clear (lob) to the rearcourt is another attacking move designed to keep the opponent away from the forecourt and out of position. It is used to create a better situation from which to make a scoring hit. So with few exceptions, even stroke-moves played in a defensive situation can be used to change it into an attacking situation, if the moves are made in accordance with the principle of attack.

Even when you are in a position to hit downwards it does not follow that you must hit downwards and attack in this way. It may be that your opponent has a strong defence and so it might be better to unsettle him first and get him out of position before making a scoring hit. Hence you might play numerous attack-clears to the rearcourt or check-smashes to the forecourt, and prolong the rallies before creating the right situation to attempt a scoring hit. This is typical in ladies' singles when the attack clear and drop shot are used frequently to move the opponent around until she is caught out of position and enable a smash to be made from a weak return to the midcourt or rearcourt.

What counts as an appropriate stroke-move in relation to the principle of attack will often be decided by what the opponent can do in the situation. For example, you could use the same move and create the same situation in different games, but it might be appropriate only in one and not the other game. Let's assume that you play opponent B. You hit the shuttle high to the backhand rearcourt. B does not play forehand smashes from this situation and has a weak backhand stroke. Thus you have placed B in a situation in which he has limited moves which are inappropriate in the situation. B can only return the shuttle high to the midcourt or hit it weakly to the forecourt. You have created a situation in which you can attack and make a scoring hit.

Now you play C, who has a powerful forehand smash from the backhand rearcourt and can play a range of stroke-moves in that situation. In this case you may have made an inappropriate move and created a situation which is to C's advantage. So although you may learn to make all the moves in a situation, the appropriateness of a move will depend on the ability of your opponent and what you can do with his reply. But, in all cases, it is only by reference to the principle of attack that you can judge how good your moves actually are.

The framework makes the game more interesting and meaningful, giving you a finer understanding of how to play it. At first you might think that if you use the framework you must spend a lot of time theorising about your move before you hit the shuttle. But players do not play the game in this way. They have neither the time nor the inclination for a quick mental rehearsal before every stroke-move. Even if the game can be seen as a form of physical chess, unlike chess there is just no time for long periods of reflection and planning during a rally. Most of the time you play intuitively and automatically without consciously thinking about each stroke-move and what the opponent is likely to do. But that does not mean that no thinking goes on. Subconsciously you are judging the situation and 'reading' the game. You do try to hit the shuttle to those places which will, you expect, gain you the advantage. You do make decisions about what is likely to work, based on your knowledge of the game gained from your experience of numerous similar situations against many different opponents. In this respect, playing badminton is like driving a car. You drive along 'reading' the activity in the road ahead of you, intuitively making decisions and responding to the situations which arise. All those decisions you 'automatically' make are a result of much learning about how to control the car, i.e. the techniques of driving, the rules of the road, and how to interpret them so that you make the correct moves in a situation. Your skill in 'reading' the road and making the appropriate moves develops as you experience many different situations in your daily driving. The big difference is that car drivers do not drive in accordance with the 'principle of attack': the results would be disastrous. You might say that what makes a move appropriate in car driving is the 'principle of safety'.

You need knowledge and much experience as a basis for what you do in the game. It is this knowledge that you use to read your opponent's game, sometimes consciously before play, and always intuitively during the game. If you do this you will automatically adapt your stroke-moves to suit different opponents in your struggle to win.

In some ways there is nothing new to be learnt from the framework. Basically, the same strokes are required and the same tactics operate. The strokes as strokes are still very important for, unless skilfully performed, they will not contribute much as tactical moves in the game. For this reason you have little option but to examine your techniques of hitting and travelling (strokes and footwork), to consider whether they are adequate to ensure that you can make the stroke-move and can recover quickly to connect one situation with another. The guide in this is the principle of attack, the rationale that underlies all the strategy and tactics in the game.

How you make use of the framework is up to you, but in placing the emphasis on the thinking in the game it offers you the opportunity for the development of tactics and strategy to a higher level of play. The game played at this level reflects our ingenuity and creative ability in devising a game designed to stretch us physically, mentally and emotionally, and provide us with a never-ending source of interest and satisfaction.

Chapter 4 Players in a Framework

It should be obvious by now that if you want to play the game successfully you must be able to make the moves to create situations to your advantage. So, amongst other aspects, you must learn a range of strokes and become skilful in your footwork.

Unfortunately, there is a tendency these days to use the strokes as strokes only without giving much thought, if any, to their use as moves in the game. In my opinion, this state is due mainly to the development of coaching in badminton. Many young players are so overcoached on strokes in stroke practices and set routines that it gets forgotten that the point of the game is to defeat the opponent, and that the strokes are simply tools used to achieve that end. A stroke in isolation may require some very skilled movement but, unless it serves its function as a move in the game, it can be wasted. Strokes seen as moves in a game are part of a pattern of moves used to create situations in which you can make a scoring hit. Out of this context a stroke is quite meaningless. In the context of a game it becomes meaningful, for as a move it is related to the preceding move and to the next move. It should never be forgotten that when you hit the shuttle it only makes sense if you relate what you do to the effect it has on the opponent. It is not strokes you play on the court; it is the opponent. That is something you must never forget. If you have a coach who does, in his struggle for stroke perfection, remind him.

Generally speaking, players vary in their use of strokes as moves in the game. The stroke-moves a player makes or doesn't make can give us an insight into his tactical thinking or lack of it. The framework enables us to assess *all* players' types of game, without exception. All players must play within the framework when performing on court according to the rules of badminton. For example, if you study different players in action you will notice that some reflect much thought during the game and make a high percentage of appropriate moves, whereas others seem to reflect little thought and mix appropriate moves with a high percentage of inappropriate moves. Different players have a differently constructed framework. This is easy to 'see' if we take our framework and compare how different players work within it. You might recognise yourself as one of them. There are three basic types: those players who appear to operate in a 'complete' framework;

those who operate in an 'incomplete' framework; and those who operate in a 'badly constructed' framework.

The complete framework

In this framework all the parts are connected to form a unified whole. We know this from what a player does. And he does nearly everything right. He can make a range of stroke-moves in a situation and is able to judge and select which one is most likely to improve his chances of winning the rally. He knows his capabilities and those of his opponent in the situation he creates. In fact his framework is well designed and very clear to him. He knows what he is doing. He sees how all the moves are related according to the principle of attack and how each contributes towards making a scoring move to win the rally.

This player may be so skilful in his strokes, footwork and use of strokes as moves that he does not really consider his opponent's game. He may play the same way every time. He plays simple 'percentage' moves, knows the obvious replies and recovers to deal with them. For example, he knows that his smash gets a lift or a block return; and that his attack clear to one side gets a clear or a drop reply and to the other side gets the smash as a reply. He knows that his drop to the forecourt gets a lift or net reply in a certain situation. There is no reply he cannot manage. He never has to take chances or make random moves. So he plays his normal game consistently at speed, with control and accuracy, making few errors and recovering into position to cover any possible reply. He gives his opponent little opportunity to make a scoring hit. This player has reached the stage where he plays without conscious thought during a game, for with regular quality practice and competitive play he has developed efficient strokes and movement and the basic tactical moves which he can maintain at high speed for long periods. Nothing really troubles him. There is very little, if anything, any other player can do that he could not immediately cope with or adapt to in the course of the game. All the pressure is on the opponent. He has to struggle to cope with this confident player.

Such a player is the champion, the best player at his particular level of play. Only when he makes continual errors or loses is he forced to examine his game. Then he works on his technique, fitness, attitude or tactics. To reach such a standard much thought and learning has taken place.

In recent years a number of players have reached this standard and dominated the game for a period. Judy Hashman (née Devlin) was the supreme player in all these respects. She has been followed by Yuki and Lena Koppen, both great tactical players with a positive attitude, who controlled opponents with the situations they created with their stroke-moves. Among the men, Erland Kops and Rudi Hartono immediately spring to mind as complete players who dominated for long periods of time because of their all-round expertise. All these players operated in a complete framework.

The incomplete framework

In this framework not all the parts are apparent to the player. He knows that there are similar situations that occur during the game and that certain moves are possible. But he has not identified all the possible situations. There are gaps in his knowledge. He has not worked out all the possible stroke-moves nor the best way to recover after making a stroke-move. Consequently, in a contest against a superior player he finds himself in two sorts of situation.

Firstly, there is the situation he is familiar with. This enables him to make stroke-moves which are sometimes appropriate and sometimes not appropriate. He may make an inappropriate move because he lacks sufficient skill or knowledge of his opponent and therefore cannot take this into account in his judgement of the situation. He needs more time to develop his technical skill and to learn about his opponent's possible replies in a situation.

Secondly, a situation he is not familiar with. This often happens against a superior opponent who creates a new situation, which he has not experienced before and so cannot identify. He becomes confused. He does not know all the possible moves nor how to perform them and so is forced to make a random move which may or may not work. If it does work then he has gained a new move appropriate to use against that opponent and, perhaps, any other opponent in the future. If it does not work he learns this quickly and can eliminate it from use should that situation occur again with that opponent.

This type of player is learning the game from first-hand experience. As he experiences a new situation he learns to identify it and can later consider the moves possible in that sort of situation. It is usually only against the superior opponent that he will find himself in situations which are new to him. Each new situation poses a problem which he has to solve by attempting to make an appropriate move. This he does by trial and error until, eventually, he learns that in a given situation certain stroke-moves work and others don't. In some games he may be successful; his random moves work and he solves the problems. But he has not yet reached the stage of the complete player who is in control of all situations and so wins consistently. Any improvement in his game can only arise from play against a superior player, for it is he who will provide him with the first-hand experience of new situations. This is one reason why he should play against many different players and many better players. Regular play in team matches, local tournaments and open tournaments is essential if you want to become a better player.

The badly constructed framework

In such a framework the player does not realise that he is in a situation because he cannot 'see' one, and does not understand that situations exist. Thus there is nothing to which he can relate; there is no guiding principle to determine whether or not certain moves are appropriate. In fact, because he cannot 'see' the situation *as* a situation he does not understand that there are moves which are appropriate in that situation, so in a sense he plays like a man who is partially blind. He sees the strokes only as strokes and not as moves in the game. Thus he is only really concerned with himself and his movements. He might possess a good range of strokes and excellent skill in travelling around the court, and he might even follow some rules in his use of strokes – but not in a way which shows he understands the reasons for the rules. For example, one international player during the build-up to the 1975 Uber Cup competition returned from the Irish Championships having lost to a player against whom we expected her to win. When I asked her about the game she told me that she had played the 'correct' game. She had hit drops and clears to the corners but it hadn't worked. This is a typical example of a player who has been taught the 'tips for singles' approach to the game. Many young players are given this sort of advice without the reasons behind the tactics. In most cases, it is doubtful whether the person giving the advice even knows the reasons when pushed to justify such advice. There is nothing wrong with hitting drops and clears to the corners if you know what sort of situation they are intended to create; when used as stroke-moves they must be hit in accordance with the principle of attack.

Another rule slavishly followed some years ago and still heard today is: 'never smash from the rearcourt in singles'. Such advice reflects a limited view of the use of the smash: the view that the smash should be used only to hit winners. But there is nothing special about the smash. It can be hit from anywhere as a stroke-move used to obtain a block or lift as a reply. It is very effective if used in this way as long as you can recover to get into position to meet the replies. If you cannot follow up and do something in the situation you have created, then you should not smash. But that advice would apply to any stroke-move. Generally speaking, you should not make any stroke-move if you cannot cover the replies. However, like any general rule, there may be exceptions to it in certain circumstances. One must always allow for the exception to the rule, otherwise we would never make progress in badminton or any other activity.

The players in the badly constructed type of framework do not use the strokes as moves in the game. Their strokes are more like conditioned responses to different stimuli. The only way that such a player can know whether he has played the right stroke is when he makes a winning hit. He may be extremely fit and possess a good range of stylish strokes but he does not connect one stroke as a move to the next stroke as a move. He has no apparent sense of purpose. So when he hits the shuttle he has to wait to see what his opponent does before he can travel to perform another stroke. It is as though he is always one move behind.

When he meets an inferior player his superior strokes can help him to win easily. However, when he meets a player of equal stroke ability who uses his strokes as moves he can lose very easily or have a hard struggle. He will rarely win. This is because he leaves it to chance whether or not his strokes are appropriate in the situations. If they are, he will have a long battle with his equal opponent, for that opponent will be able to contend with most of the situations. If his strokes are not appropriate then he will lose easily. He cannot control the play, for there is no clear purpose to his play. He plays a type of game which is difficult to explain, and makes many rash shots and careless errors.

There is no doubt that such a player can suffer. Dismay, confusion, helplessness, frustration and anger are all part of his act when he does lose to anyone he considers less than his outright superior. His court behaviour shows it well. It is not unusual to see such a player swearing, racket throwing, sulking, giving up, arguing with officials, as he questions decisions and so on. Blaming everyone and everything except himself, he cannot understand how, with such technical skill, he can lose. He simply forgets that the game requires more than the ability to hit a shuttle. He has yet to learn what it actually means to play opponents and not simply play strokes. Against the superior opponent he will rarely have a good contest and certainly never win. For his development into the higher levels of play is dependent upon him seeing the strokes as moves in a situation played in accordance with the principle of attack.

The three types of player as reflected in these frameworks are not so easily identified in practice as I have described them here. They are models. However, there are many players who fit into these different frameworks at various times. I am sure that you will be able to identify yourself among them. The important lesson to learn is that more understanding of the game can be gained from looking at yourself and other players in terms of our framework. It should help you to assess your game and so identify what you should learn to improve it. It will certainly help you to assess your opponent's game and work out some moves which could contribute towards your success in competition. Don't forget that the game is a contest and the point of the game is to win. Thus, if a game is played in accordance with the principle of attack, every stroke-move must contribute to that attack. Only in this way will you play purposefully towards winning.

Part Two

Performance in the Game

Chapter 5 Performance in the Game

What you must learn to play singles

A study of the charts would seem to imply that there is much you must learn to perform competently in singles. These things can be listed as follows:

1. You must learn the various techniques of hitting the shuttle, i.e. the strokes and the variations on the strokes. You should then be able to hit the shuttle from anywhere in your court to anywhere in your opponent's court to make the moves in the situation.

2. You must learn how to travel from one situation to another, position yourself to hit the shuttle, and recover from that stroke-move to travel into a new position in time to cover the possible replies. To do this requires skilful footwork and good balance.

3. You must be able to meet the physical demands of the game. Any fitness training must be designed to improve your ability to travel easily between situations and to perform moves in those situations. The fitness training must link up with travelling and hitting techniques. This is achieved by continuous work over a period of time.

4. You must learn to make the appropriate stroke-moves. Thus you must learn all the stroke-moves possible in a situation. Then you can learn what is appropriate by finding out what is actually possible for you and your opponent. To do this you require more knowledge of your own game and that of your opponent. If in a given situation there are ten moves possible and your opponent can only make four of those moves then you can plan accordingly and create situations to your advantage. The framework provides you with a checklist of possible moves, their replies and how to recover after making a move. You can assess what you or your opponent can do against that check list. If you find that you have any weakness, then you can devise practices to correct that weakness. For example, let us assume that you never quite manage to recover to meet the 'block' reply at the top of the net after you have travelled backwards to smash from the rearcourt. More often than not, by the time you reach the shuttle, it has fallen near the floor in the forecourt. Consequently the situation is to your disadvantage and often results in your losing the rally. You might not realise that, ideally, you ought to

take the shuttle at the top of the net after your smash from the rearcourt. If you are not aware of this, the framework will indicate it, for it provides a list of possibilities in any situation. One reason for using the smash as a tactical move is to obtain the block reply to the forecourt so that you are able to travel forwards and attack the shuttle at the top of the net. You can always learn what you ought to try to achieve with your stroke-moves by referring to the framework. In this case, you must work out why you are unable to travel forwards in time to take the shuttle near the top of the net and not near the floor. There could be several reasons. It could be the way you approach the forecourt to make your stroke-move; your footwork or stroke technique might be inadequate; it could be that you step backwards after the smash because you did not get into the smash position to begin with, and thus are slow to recover to reach the replies to the forecourt. When you have decided what the cause is, you can devise a practice which will include travelling backwards to get into the smash position, the stroke-move and the recovery to enable you to travel to meet the shuttle near the top of the net.

From this brief discussion it is clear that much must be learnt if you want to improve your performance and become a complete player. If this is the case, then you should be clear just what aspects of your performance you want or need to improve. So let us take a closer look at performance and see what it implies for you in the game.

Performance and standards

A lot can be gained from exploring 'performance' in some depth. In this context, this word is used in two ways, both of which are important in your development as a singles player.

First, we can talk about a successful or unsuccessful performance when we refer simply to whether you won or lost the game. We simply state a fact about the result of the game, e.g. 'John gave a successful performance', meaning that John won the game. (This doesn't tell us very much and isn't really interesting.) Second, we can say that John gave a good or a poor performance, regardless of whether or not John won or lost the game. (It is quite usual for a player to come off court and be told that he has played well, even though he has lost.) In fact there would be no contradiction in saying that John lost but gave a good performance, or John won but played badly.

You must understand in what sense your performance is good or bad, quite apart from the result of the match, or you learn nothing and make no progress. Progress in singles is very much dependent on learning and you should learn something about your performance as a player each time you play a game. But this is only true if you are able to evaluate how you played in the game. Comments of the 'good' and 'bad' type are judgements about the value of your performance with respect to standards of excellence in some aspect of the game: the suggestion is that your performance either comes up to standard or falls below that standard in some way.

Nevertheless, even though it is important that you attain good standards in performance, it is even more important that you are successful in the game. Winning is what the game is all about. Hence successful performance is the main target. The ideal state, obviously, is to give a performance which is both good and successful. You should try to win and also attain the desired standards of excellence within the game. In fact, the chances of success are increased if you can also ensure a good standard of performance.

At this point the framework becomes useful in identifying these inter-related features of performance and demonstrating the standards of excellence you should try to attain. It contains the sum total of all those aspects of the game you must learn in order to become a singles player: the framework is the game.

The framework serves as a measure by which you can assess your knowledge and understanding, simply by comparing what you can do with what you ought to do to reach the highest standard of performance possible, i.e. *perfection*. This is personified in the notion of the 'complete player': one who reaches the highest standard in all aspects of the game and so wins unless equalled by any opponent. Of course, in a sense, perfection is an unattainable ideal, even though it is the distant destination you seek if you want to become a better player; for to seek perfection is to seek the standards of excellence (what counts as 'good'), in the various parts that make up performance.

We also have a further set of related standards. These are the practical standards of performance set by different opponents at different levels of play within the game. These we can quite easily recognise, for they range between those of the beginner and of the current world champion. Between these two levels are a number of steps which must be climbed, each one more difficult and demanding. It is possible to compare progress in the different levels of play with climbing a pyramid (see fig. 7). There are many routes up the pyramid and the choice of route and method of travel will depend on the way the game is organised in different countries throughout the world. Obviously at some stage one needs access to international tourna-ment play to become a valid contender for the title of world champion. It is most unlikely that a player could become successful at that level of play unless he had also attained high standards of excellence in all the various parts of the game.

These levels of play are very important, for they give you the chance to test your progress on your journey to becoming a better player. However good your practical knowledge of what stroke-moves to perform and theoretical knowledge of when they are appropriate in a situation, there

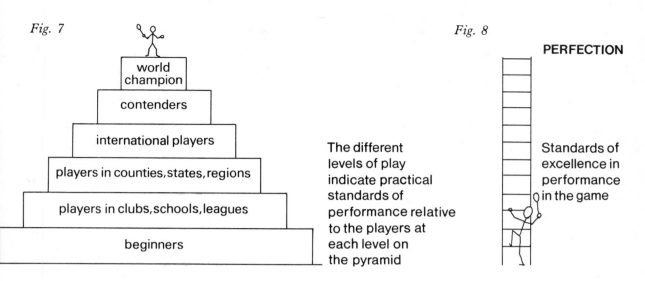

Fig. 7

world champion

contenders

international players

players in counties, states, regions

players in clubs, schools, leagues

beginners

The different levels of play indicate practical standards of performance relative to the players at each level on the pyramid

Fig. 8

PERFECTION

Standards of excellence in performance in the game

comes the time when you must try out your knowledge on the court. The test is to compete against other players. If you can progress from club player to the club team and win the club singles championship you have become a better player. From there you can continue to progress, becoming the best at each level and gradually a better player. Note that 'better' here is not only relative to other players, and levels of play set by those players. Each opponent at each level of play is a test of your progress, not only towards the top of the players' pyramid but also towards the ideal of perfection. This ideal, with its objective standards of excellence within the different parts of the game, runs parallel to the pyramid though separate from it (see fig. 8). The objective standards of excellence are quite different from the practical standards set by players.* Even the world champion, who is on top of the

---

* For example, the intention of the clear as a stroke-move is to get the shuttle over the opponent's head and make him travel to the rearcourt. There are several sets of standards involved here; with respect to the way you hit the shuttle, a good standard of skilled performance would be described in terms of smooth, fluent, economical, rhythmic, neat and efficient stroke production. The shuttle would be hit with control to travel accurately to the desired place in the rearcourt. As a stroke-move it would be of a good standard only if it caught the opponent out, i.e. made him late getting to the rearcourt, made him travel all the way to the rearcourt, reduced his chances of making a scoring hit, and created a situation to your advantage.

These are objective standards of good performance determined by the nature of the game and what good players at the highest level are capable of achieving consistently in the game. Practical standards of performance are relative to the various levels of player in the game. Two beginners may use the clear as a move but perform it technically with excessive movement and inefficient production of the stroke. Consequently it does not send the opponent to the rearcourt. Nevertheless it could still be effective as a move at that level of play because the opponent, as a beginner, may find that even such a crude clear is to his disadvantage. Although we recognise that beginners are well below the objective standard of what counts as 'good', when compared with the standards set within the framework and the ultimate ideal of 'perfection', they are capable of playing below this standard and still attaining the practical standards relative to their level of play. At their level this would be sufficient to win the game.

pyramid, can still work towards the ideal of perfection as set out in the framework, and become a better player in the sense of becoming a more complete player. Indeed he must do so, for if he rests on his laurels he risks losing the title of best player. In defeating an opponent, he unavoidably 'teaches' that opponent about his (the champion's) game and also about the opponent's own game. Hence an intelligent and ambitious contender will begin to do whatever is necessary to eliminate weaknesses and devise ways to improve his standards of performance in the various aspects of the game. So the next time he meets the champion he will be better equipped to challenge the champion for his title. No champion can afford to stand still. Like all players, he must aim at the twin targets necessary in any progress towards becoming a better player. These are, again, the ideal of perfection inherent in the framework which is personified in the complete player; and the intervening targets of the different levels of player (though in the world champion's case his only threat is from the contenders in the pyramid).

To sum up briefly: you test yourself against other players to measure your progress on the road to perfection (the unattainable ideal); and to help you there is the framework, which makes it possible to test and measure yourself accurately and also provides the means of improving your performance, giving a frame of reference to assess any aspect of your performance in the game. The task now is to take a closer look at the different aspects of performance and try to work out the desired standards of excellence inherent in each part.

The components of performance

Performance comprises three main components. These are skill, fitness and attitude. I shall discuss only skill and fitness here, and attitude, the most complex component, separately in Chapter Six.

1. Skill Skill consists of the technical and tactical aspects of performance.

a. Technical skill

The technical aspects are the strokes and footwork, i.e. the various techniques of hitting the shuttle and travelling from one situation to another to hit the shuttle. The emphasis here is on the art of moving in the game. This is most apparent if you reflect upon the descriptions used about various skilful players. We talk about the strokes in terms of a 'powerful' smash, a 'gentle' dropshot; he 'caresses' the shuttle over the net, and possesses a 'flashing' backhand. In these instances we refer to the way a player hits the shuttle and use various aesthetic words to paint a picture of the impression we receive. The same can be said of the general movement around the court when we refer to the player as graceful, flowing, gliding, skimming the ground and landing featherlight.

In using such descriptions, not only do we paint a picture of the player in action but also evaluate the way he performs and suggest therefore that he comes up to some standard of excellence that we admire and enjoy. Usually we are even more specific than this and refer to stroke production as neat, tidy, economical in time and energy (all necessary to hit the shuttle with control and accuracy). The footwork and general movement we refer to as balanced, quick, light and controlled. Here we are more concerned with the mechanical efficiency of the technical performance than with the beauty of the performance. The descriptions we generally use are a combination of physical and aesthetic descriptions which sometimes overlap, as when we use the word 'powerful' which tells us something about the force used to hit the shuttle and the quality of the movement of the player in his execution of the stroke. Both types of description imply that there are standards of performance which we believe are the mark of a good player. A player must become very proficient in using his racket, and in his footwork and general movement about the court. It is worth taking a closer look at the techniques of hitting and moving in the game.

Hitting and moving techniques

Badminton is a hitting game which involves the delivery of 'blows' to an opponent. There is, of course, no physical contact with the opponent, for you hit the shuttle not the opponent. Nevertheless, the game involves the aggressive element of attack. The racket is the weapon that delivers the 'blow'. The game is played at speed, making quick recovery after the blow essential. The rule to follow is 'hit and move'. Balance and control are important factors in recovery. A player who travels to a situation to make a stroke-move and loses balance will be slow to recover. Poor hitting and travelling techniques can upset balance and slow the recovery. Correct hitting and moving techniques appropriate to the stroke-move in the situation are necessary.

Hitting techniques

The badminton racket is very light and can be used very easily to apply much force with a minimum of strength and movement. There are a number of different grips which allow you to hold the racket in different ways to hit the shuttle in various situations. The grip serves two functions. First, it enables you to control the racket face and so direct the shuttle to any place in the opponent's court. Second, it enables you to control the racket head to apply more or less force to the shuttle in the chosen direction. You can read about the grips and strokes in my earlier books *Badminton for Schools* and *Better Badminton for All* (both published by Pelham Books Ltd).

The racket should be held in position ready to hit the shuttle from anywhere in the space around the body. For rearcourt moves, the racket is simply lifted back and held ready to hit the shuttle from a high position (see plate 22). The force of the blow will be determined by the weight and speed of the racket head. With a light racket head you will need to generate more speed. One possible way is by holding the racket near the bottom of the handle, thus effectively increasing the length of the racket (see plate 23), and by keeping your trunk still during the hitting phase of the action. This will also assist balance and recovery.

In the forecourt and midcourt less movement of the arm is required since the blow will usually require less force. Nevertheless, the trunk must be in a

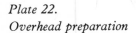

Plate 22.
Overhead preparation

Plate 23.
Long grip

Plate 24.
Short grip

state of balance to allow you to deliver quick 'blows' in the forecourt and midcourt. It helps here to shorten the length of the racket by holding it near the top of the handle (see plate 24), and then the 'blow' and recovery are more rapid.

The trunk acts as the main axis around which the blows are delivered. It remains firm and fixed whilst blows are delivered with various degrees of force to the shuttle located in different areas of space around it. It is quite easy to experience this. Take your racket, stand with your feet firmly planted and tense the muscles in your thighs and bottom. Then allowing only your shoulders to rotate when necessary, hit the space around the body with a series of rapid strong blows. There is little time – nor is more necessary – for a large 'preparation' or 'follow-through' after each blow. Now repeat the exercise whilst delivering soft 'blows'. Excess movement is eliminated and greater efficiency is obtained. The movements are perfectly natural and sufficient for the job. The general rule is not to use more movement and energy than is necessary to make a particular stroke-move.

You can gain further insight into hitting techniques with a study of karate, boxing, aikido and kendo. Most sports centres offer such activities and there is an excellent opportunity to watch the athletes in training and practice, which is the best time to watch, for then they tend to repeat the same actions continuously. In these activities balance and speed of recovery are crucial. Thus these sports develop certain techniques and special exercises designed to increase the speed of hitting and recovery with the minimum of movement. The preparation for the 'blow' does not just involve physical readiness but also mental readiness. The force originates in the centre of the body and generates rapidly (sometimes explosively) outwards into the 'blow'. To achieve this effect the attention is focused on the moment of the 'blow'. This requires concentration of thought with movement. It does not matter whether the blow is soft or strong, the same attention must be focused on that moment in time when the racket strikes the shuttle. To do this takes much hard work and repetition in the early stages of learning. You have to develop a quality of movement in your hitting technique. For speed of hitting and recovery with control partly depends on your ability to tense and relax muscles rapidly. When you hit quickly, the muscles must be able to contract rapidly. (This is the 'tension'.) Rapid contraction can, however, only come from relaxed muscles. (This is the 'relaxation'.) If the tension involves strain, this simply implies the inability to relax muscles properly in the first place. 'Tension' and 'relaxation' are the basis of speed and control. The quality of such movement requires a large degree of mental control, and a conscious awareness and control over the bodily state. A simple experiment will confirm this. Try the following exercises.

Body awareness

Stand upright with feet shoulder width apart. Allow your shoulders to slump and your arms to hang heavily; collapse rather than relax. Now imagine that you are connected to the electricity supply. It is switched on and a very low voltage is passed through your body – just sufficient to alert your muscles. There is a very light tension throughout your body. Begin to straighten up. Allow your arms to remain by your sides. Focus your attention on the tension in the fingers until they feel light and alert, without strain. Hold the increased tension and experience the power and energy available. Now the voltage is gradually reduced and the tension reduces until you feel it very lightly in the fingertips. Concentrate and maintain the light tension throughout your whole body. Hold it for a moment and then let the shoulders collapse. The current has been turned off. Begin again. The current is turned on. You go into a state of light tension. Feel it in the fingertips. Bend your arms so that your hands are held lightly in front of you. Imagine the voltage is increased very rapidly for a fraction of a second. In that time you make a rapid blow with an increase in tension and then as the voltage decreases, reduce the tension and remain with your arms bent and hands in front ready to make another blow. Now perform a series of quick blows and then each time reduce the voltage so that you return to a state of light tension throughout the body, felt particularly in the fingers and hands.

At no time does the current get turned off. The body is always held in a state of light tension (relaxation phase), ready to travel and hit the shuttle. Then the tension increases and reduces when the work has been completed. There is no sign of collapse throughout the body in a single muscle during the actual play. Unfortunately, many players lack this quality of movement in their actions. They collapse in the back muscles after a smash so the trunk falls forwards after the stroke-move. The arm collapses after a gentle net reply (a soft 'blow'). The upper body collapses and goes heavy after a backward jump smash or after a lunge in the forecourt. Hence control and balance are poor; recovery is slow and unnecessarily energy-consuming, and the player is unable to cover the replies to his stroke-move with maximum effect.

All the strength, speed and agility that comes from fitness training will not improve the quality of movement unless you are aware of the sensation of tension and relaxation in your muscles and can control that state through-out your performance. The same quality of movement is required in your technique of travelling over the court to make the stroke-moves. Here you must be able to travel easily and quickly from one situation to another. And in this respect good posture and carriage in conjunction with good footwork is most important. If the trunk rests lightly and balances easily on the hips without strain then it becomes easier to travel around the court. The legs will have less work to do, for the trunk 'rides' on them without being a burden to them. You will understand what I mean if you have ever given anyone a 'piggy back' ride and they have let their weight go and become heavy – a 'dead weight' – on your back. It is quite a burden to carry around. It is less so if the 'rider' holds himself up and carries some of his own weight. He appears to make himself lighter and consequently you can move around more easily. Similarly in play, if you carry your trunk lightly on your legs, you will be able to travel around the court easily and without strain. The tactical benefits of good technique with quality of movement are seen in less time taken to travel to the shuttle and to recover from your stroke-move to cover the reply, and even greater control and accuracy in the execution of the stroke-move. Thus you can maintain an effective attack.

Plate 25.
Backward jump

Travelling techniques

The means of travel between situations can vary. Between the midcourt and the rearcourt it usually takes the form of sprints, sidesteps and jumps (see plate 25). This is performed lightly and with a softness of foot which improves the speed of travel and indicates a concern for quality of movement in the body. The action of accelerating from a particular stance, e.g. defensive, is achieved by bending the knees and lowering the upright body and then using the strong thigh muscles and muscles of the lower leg and foot to push rapidly into the floor to thrust you away from the spot (see plate 26). Similarly, the ability to stop quickly in balance requires the use of

Plate 26.
Acceleration

the same muscle groups in the legs to act as brakes and allow you to make the stroke-move before thrusting you away again as you push off to recover and travel for a new situation. The speed of travel, and starting and stopping, is dependent on the relationship between the trunk and the legs and the overall quality of muscular tension in the body.

The means of travel between the midcourt and the forecourt is either by taking steps to travel up to the shuttle to arrive in balance (see plate 27), or by stretching to extend the reach. The most common action is the lunge, similar to that used by the fencer, and an action that maintains the body in balance and aids speedier recovery. With training and an awareness of posture and balance you should learn to stretch into a deep lunge at speed

Plate 27.
Balanced forecourt stance

with maximum control and possess the strength and technique to recover smoothly from the lunge with control.

Any training in travelling around the court should include:

a. Pushing off quickly from the spot with short sprints in backward, forward and diagonal directions to stop quickly in balance and then push off to recover.

b. Sidesteps towards the corners with a jump to smash and then a controlled landing before pushing away to recover.

c. Exercises designed to increase flexibility in the legs, hip joint and lower back to ensure the ability to perform full deep lunges in forward and sideways directions whilst the trunk remains centred and in balance (see plates 28 and 29). For those players interested in this aspect of performance, I

Plate 28.
Forward lunge

Plate 29.
Side lunge

would recommend some study and observation of contemporary and classical dance training methods and also Olympic gymnastic stretching exercises. In addition, careful observation of fencers and top-class badminton players will provide some insight into the technical aspects of hitting and travelling in the game.

b. Tactical skill

By this, we mean the use of stroke-moves to defeat the opponent. The emphasis is solely on how an opponent is played. When we describe and evaluate the tactical aspect of performance we tend to apply words concerned with mental powers. A good player in this respect reaches a high standard if he uses common sense, plays intelligently, is shrewd or cunning, imaginative and creative. These are the standards we want the good player to achieve. Hence to become a better player you must make stroke-moves which are appropriate in the situations that occur during a rally. Then, and only then, can you be said to have reached the desired tactical standards and to deserve such descriptions as 'intelligent' and 'imaginative'. To reach the desired standards in the technical and tactical aspects of skilled performance requires much work in practice and competition; how to work in these areas is discussed in more detail in Chapter Eight.

The technical and tactical skill required are clearly shown in the charts. Skill in playing requires a combination of both in the form of stroke-moves played in situations in accordance with the principle of attack. To ensure a good performance there are various standards expressed in physical, mental and aesthetic judgements of performance that the execution of a stroke and the choice of a stroke-move must attain. If you want to become a better player with respect to skilled performance then you must look critically at your performance in these terms.

2. Fitness

Fitness is a difficult word to explain for it is used to describe both physical and mental states. For instance, a person who 'feels' fit can be proved not at all fit by a few minutes' hard exercise, while a highly trained player who is superbly fit can go on court and not feel fit.

As these examples show, we use the word to refer to both our mental state of well-being and our physical state. The purpose of being fit is to improve our capacity for hard physical work and to delay the onset of and quicken the recovery from fatigue. Here we are concerned mainly with fitness specifically for badminton, with respect to physical performance in the game and, to some extent, with 'feeling' fit to play the game.

If you cannot do the work required, i.e. the amount of work at the rate the game is being played, then your technical and tactical performance will suffer. You will fall below your standards in stroke production and become inefficient, make errors and lose accuracy and control. You might also begin to make errors in judgement and 'read' the game badly.

No matter how intelligent you are as a player, if your moves do not create the situations you intend because the shuttle does not go where you aim it, you will reduce your chances of winning. In addition, if you are too tired to get into position to cover the replies in the situations you create, then you will obviously lose any advantage you have played for and may perhaps lose the rally. It is easy to see that your skill and fitness are separate but inter-dependent aspects of your performance. So also are attitude and fitness. It is most important that, if you have trained hard and achieved a high standard of fitness, you should actually 'feel' fit when you step onto the court. It would be most disappointing to feel listless, lethargic, tired and drained of all energy, and this can happen if you are not in the right state of mind before and during the game. How you can prevent this happening or overcome it when it does happen is a difficult problem to solve. In fact there are few positive solutions though there are many suggestions, some of which work and others of which do not. In Chapter Six, when 'attitude' is considered, I shall discuss this in more depth to provide some understanding of how it is caused and how it relates to your performance in the game. At this point it is sufficient to indicate that 'attitude' is related to fitness as a factor in your performance.

a. Fitness components

There are a number of fitness components that you must develop. These are: agility, flexibility, local muscular and cardio-vascular endurance, strength, power, speed and the correct maintenance of body weight.

Agility is the ability to change direction quickly with control whilst travelling at speed. This is something you must be able to do in the game as you travel from one situation to another during a rally.

Flexibility is the ability to extend your limbs through the full range of movement required to meet all the twisting and turning and stretching that the game demands.

Local muscular endurance is the ability to use the same group of muscles continuously without fatigue, e.g. when you have to perform many overhead strokes or travel backwards and forwards throughout the game. If your legs begin to feel heavy or it becomes a strain to make that overhead clear then it could be that the muscle groups involved are suffering from fatigue. You are not fit enough to do that amount of work. This is a good example of how lack of fitness can affect your skill.

Cardio-vascular endurance is the capacity to keep up demanding activity over long periods of time, particularly when it involves large muscle groups. The popular name for this component is 'heart and lungs' endurance, because it is involved with the transportation of energy to the working muscles. As badminton demands much running and jumping you will need a constant supply of energy to those heavily worked muscles. This will only come about if the heart and lungs are capable of working efficiently for long stretches of time.

Strength is to do with the amount of force you can exert with your muscles and relates closely to *power*, which is the capacity to release the maximum force in the shortest possible time. A powerful player is one who not only is strong but can exert that force very quickly, almost explosively. The Indonesian player Lien Swie King is an excellent example of this, possessing tremendous power which is seen clearly when he springs upwards to smash (see plate 30.)

Plate 30.
Liem Swie King
power jump

Speed is simply the ability to run fast and move quickly from one place to another. It links up with power for, in the game, speed of acceleration is usually dependent on power. This is seen when you have to explode from a defensive stance to reach an attack clear early enough to reply with a smash.

Maintenance of correct body weight is important to ensure that you do not do more work than is necessary, but are capable of doing all that is necessary. Thus, if you are overweight you carry an extra load and must do more work to carry yourself around. This uses up vital energy. If you are below your correct weight it is most likely that you will be either too weak to do the work or not have sufficient energy stored in the body. Correct body weight is maintained through a combination of exercise and diet.

On getting fit

There are three essential factors which contribute to badminton fitness. These are:

1. *Training.* The fitness components are developed by training the body in various ways to withstand the rigours of the game. The type of work done in training should, as much as is possible, relate to the type of physical movement you will actually perform in the game. The best training will occur on court, performing strokes and stroke-moves in selected situations.
2. *Rest.* A certain amount of rest is important to allow the body to recover from the work. This includes the rest taken during training and the rest gained between training sessions doing other things or in natural sleep.
3. *Diet.* A correct diet ensures that the body is supplied with the essential fuel to meet the demands of play, and that correct body weight is maintained.

It is very important in any training programme that you get the balance right between these factors. This is essential if there is to be any improvement in fitness.

b. Fitness standards

The standards within fitness are to some extent built into the fitness components. The fit player should be strong, fast, powerful, agile, flexible, tireless (endurance), lean, athletic and muscular. In addition there are links with aesthetic standards with respect to the quality of movement. We might also expect the fit player to be dynamic and explosive.

The standards the fit player should attain are necessary to meet the demands of the game. Some of these standards are measurable, e.g. strength, power, speed, flexibility and the other fitness components. The aesthetic standards are not measurable in the same way for they refer to the quality of the player's fitness rather than the level of his fitness. But such aesthetic standards of fitness are dependent on the physical measurable aspects of fitness. A higher level of fitness is often reflected in a better quality of fitness shown in movement around the court. This is to be expected, for if this fitness is specific to badminton and one becomes badminton-fit by training on those movements, then necessarily one is going to become a better (more skilful) mover in the game. Thus the quality of the fitness is related to the quality of the skilled movement in the game. Fitness and skill are inseparable in the performance of quality movement which attains aesthetic standards.

The significance of these fitness standards is that they are aims for any player who wants to become better in terms of becoming a more complete player, as well as wanting to climb the pyramid into the higher levels of play. They are necessary standards for they arise from the demands of the game as reflected in the framework.

c. Training for fitness

Though it is not the intention in this book to discuss specific training methods it is possible to provide additional guidelines to getting fit. There are a number of principles you ought to consider in training for fitness. These are:

1. Build up a *general* level of fitness, i.e. an efficient cardio-vascular system.
2. Train *specifically* for badminton and so develop badminton fitness.
3. *Overload* the training. Do more work in training than the game demands.
4. Make the training *progressive*. Getting fit is a gradual business and you must build up slowly to larger amounts of work.
5. *Measure* your progress. Test yourself and then keep a record to see how you are improving.
6. Make the work interesting. Some *variety* is important.

If you want to train seriously for badminton fitness then you will find *Get Fit for Badminton* by J. Downey and D. Brodie (Pelham Books, 1980) most helpful.

Finally, even though fitness training appears to be hard work (the principle of overload and progression) it can still be enjoyable. For most sportsmen and women it can become a regular part of their daily lives. Eventually, the beneficial effect of regular training and a concern for the quality of movement in play will improve your badminton fitness. The reward comes both from the experience of the training and the end result, a better performance in the game.

Chapter 6 Attitude in Performance

Introduction

Attitude is by far the most complex aspect of performance and is inextricably bound up with skill and fitness in contributing to good performance. It is relatively easy for any keen and enthusiastic player to attain a high standard of fitness and technical skill with hard work and then, with a sound knowledge and understanding of the tactical moves and experience in competition, proceed to reach a high tactical standard. There are many players who have reached high standards in all these aspects but fail to realise their potential and gain success, solely because of their inappropriate attitude before and during a game. This problem does not only apply to players who have reached high standards of performance within the framework and operate at high levels of play on the pyramid (see fig. 7). Players at all levels and of all ages can suffer from an attitude which is inappropriate to the game. As spectators, we see many examples of this in those players who stop trying, lose their tempers, sulk, throw the racket around, argue with officials, play wildly and make numerous errors, become tense and play tentatively, lose easily when leading and in sight of victory, play too safe and do not go for the chances. In addition to these public examples of attitude there is also the player's private experience during the game to consider. You may have experienced some of these examples yourself or have been told about them by other players. Typical examples here are the players who experience doubts and fears, think about other things, find their legs feeling weak and jelly-like, cannot get a full breath, don't take that extra step because it will hurt, question the point of trying any more, get embarrassed to be seen chasing the shuttle when caught out of position, worry about what others might say if they lose, worry about winning again, think about what they will do when they have won, feel their side of the court is the size of a desert and the other side looks like a postage stamp. These are all experiences of a negative kind and will obviously affect the quality of performance and reduce the chances of winning. There are also inner experiences of a positive kind during a game. Typical of these are when you 'see' something in the opponent's expression and just 'know' that you have got him; when you are losing and just 'know' that you will win; when your side of the court seems like a postage stamp and the other side looks like a desert; when the shuttlecock appears like an enormous parachute travelling in slow motion; when you feel in complete harmony within yourself and just cannot make an error; when you feel lost in the moment and everything feels effortless; when you feel that there is nothing that you cannot do. These are all examples of inner experiences of a positive or negative kind which are private to the player. Spectators cannot see these and so really cannot know of them unless the player voices them later.

When the attitude is positive and appropriate to the game we might not give a thought to the player's private experience. We just assume that everything is going well and he is getting on with the game just as he should. But even though we don't know what sort of thoughts or feelings the player is privately experiencing we do 'know' what sort of attitude he is expressing. We will know that it is a positive one and apparently appropriate to the game because we can see that the player is expressing determination, concentration and other features of positive behaviour. It is only when the attitude appears to be negative and inappropriate, which we judge from the way he is playing as compared with how we think he ought to play (as against objective standards within a framework), that we reflect upon his experience. We become curious, to say the least, about why he plays in such a way. We wonder about the cause of such behaviour, in terms of what he is thinking about and what he is actually experiencing. Sometimes the player can tell us and sometimes he doesn't even know himself what he was experiencing to cause the negative inappropriate behaviour which affected his performance. He just knows that something went wrong. If he does know what he was experiencing, e.g. some worry about what others would say if he lost, he may not know why he did or should worry about what others might say. All he knows is that at 12–12 in the final set he began to make mistakes and as always did not know why.

Even in this brief discussion, it will have become apparent that attitude is a complex and difficult area to understand, for it includes the feelings and emotions of the players. One cannot learn and develop attitudes in the same way one can develop physical skills and fitness. What makes it more difficult is that there appear to be several levels of experience which can affect a player's attitude. These are, first, the *private inner experience* of the player in which he feels or thinks in positive or negative ways before and during the game; and second, the *public expression* of those feelings and thoughts seen in positive and negative behaviour. It is possible for a player to have negative thoughts during the game, e.g. fear of losing because of what people might say, and yet to express in his observable behaviour tremendous determination, control and concentration. In such a case we would not even suspect that a player was experiencing fear. If we did we would be amazed and admire his courage in being able to overcome his fear. Of course, the player also has positive private experiences and expresses positive attitudes in his observable behaviour.

inner private negative experience ⎯⎯ negative public behaviour

inner private positive experience ⎯⎯ positive public behaviour

We can explain attitude at the inner, private, individual level and at the outer, public, observable behavioural level. Obviously, the desirable state is for a player to have a positive inner experience and to show in his public behaviour the sort of positive attitude which is appropriate to the game, and will contribute to his performance and increase his chances of winning. It would be useful to know how those players who manage to show a positive attitude during play do so when having a negative private experience. What we also need to know and understand is how to help those players who during the game express a negative inappropriate attitude arising from a private negative experience. The main problem here is to discover the reason for the private negative experience.

There is nothing new about these questions for they have been the subject of continual study by sports psychologists. Nevertheless, as attitude plays a crucial part in performance in the game it is important to understand what it is and its place in performance.

The following discussion will consider what attitudes are appropriate, what actually does go on in the game, and how it is possible to promote appropriate attitudes. Finally, I shall discuss the possible causes of an inappropriate attitude and what can be done, either to prevent players developing such attitudes, or to alter them if they are already part of a player's behaviour.

The appropriate attitude to the game

Attitude refers to a player's behaviour. If it comes up to the recognised standard then there should be a good performance. So far I have simply stated that certain attitudes are appropriate and others not. The basis for saying that certain attitudes are appropriate is because they are logically intrinsic to the game. Such attitudes will result in behaviour which is acceptable within the game. For example, if a player adopts an attitude of fairness, he will not try to cheat his opponent. We must examine the game itself to find out what sort of attitude is appropriate to it. Let's see what conclusions we can arrive at.

It seems safe to assume that you have taken up the game voluntarily. You haven't been forced to play it; you play it because you want to. If so, it would seem that you believe that it is a worthwhile game to play and that, primarily, you value it for the enjoyment you get from playing it, solely for its intrinsic value – that is, for what is in the game for its own sake and not for some extrinsic reason such as money, travel, status amongst your friends, or because it will please someone. Later we shall see that playing for these latter sorts of reasons can lead to all kinds of problems and inappropriate attitudes.

The enjoyment can come from the exercise, the hitting of shuttles, general movement about the court, the challenge of the contest and the fact that you find it an absorbing and interesting game to play. And if you are keen and want to become a better player you will work seriously to improve your performance for the added enjoyment that comes from getting further into the game. At that point, it will become *your* game, and then you will begin to care about how you play and take some pride in your performance and the success you achieve. In which case you will be more ready to commit yourself to those standards of excellence within the different aspects of performance in the game, i.e. skill, fitness and attitude. At this stage you could be said to have a love of the game solely for the interest and enjoyment it provides.

As you continue to play and gain experience you will try to improve your skill and fitness and give little thought to your attitude. In all probability, if you play the game for its own sake, then you already have an inherent appropriate attitude; this would arise naturally owing to the nature of the game. For the game is a contest in which you and your opponent compete to win; winning is the point of the game. It is because you both try to win that the game becomes interesting, for then you can test your performance against another player. That takes time, for badminton is a game that goes on for a period of time and calls for a certain degree of skill to defeat the opponent. You will find that the game becomes absorbing as you struggle to find ways to overcome your opponent and win the contest. We might presume, therefore, that you are interested in and committed to the task of winning. To do this requires a certain degree of persistence in your efforts until the game is over. At the same time, being committed, you will try seriously to win, and will show some determination to do so. Such a commitment will demand your full concentration as you give all your attention to the task of defeating your opponent. We might conclude, at this point, that certain attitudes are expected from you if you really can claim to play the game as a contest.

There is a further source of attitudes which arises from the fact that you are playing the game with another person. The implications of this are most important, for they also determine the manner in which you play. These are the moral attitudes which arise because badminton is a game which belongs within the world of sport. Man has devised various sports throughout his history and has done so, with few exceptions, for the purpose of his enjoyment and to enhance the quality of his life in some way. In sport we enjoy many things: the competition, the challenge, the test of skill and courage, the physical movement and so on. All the different activities within sport have some point to them. The point of mountain climbing may be to 'get to the top' or to test skill and courage on a new, difficult route; of archery, to hit the target accurately; and of games, to win. The enjoyment comes from taking part, in competing against self, others or some natural challenge to succeed in the aim of that particular sport. Fundamentally, the main point of sport is enjoyment and consequently one should not try to win at the expense of the enjoyment. Any behaviour that lessens the enjoyment of sport in any way is undesirable and should, if possible, be avoided. We therefore need to know just what sort of attitudes would be appropriate in this respect.

We can start by recognising that sport is a part of the life of man and the game of badminton, a sport which involves playing against other persons. Hence social relationships with others occur and these presuppose certain *moral* considerations governing the behaviour of players towards each other and anyone else involved in the game. Morality is essentially concerned with how people behave towards each other in all aspects of life. It determines what sort of attitude is appropriate to others in the game. Hence it would be expected that a player should show some respect for the opponent, fairness, honesty and consideration for his interests in the game. When people make requests for 'sportsmanship', and the game to be played in the right spirit, they are making an appeal that morality shall prevail. And rightly so, for in such a context moral attitudes are as much a part of behaviour in the game as determination, concentration, courage and so on. Badminton is a part of the world of sport and has something to do with enhancing the quality of some part of our lives. If not, the game would hardly seem to be worth playing.

This part of the discussion can be summarised by concluding that certain attitudes are logically inherent in the game and act as the appropriate standards which a player should try to attain in order to improve the 'attitude' aspect of his performance in the game. They are care, pride in performance, a love of the game, commitment to the standards, concentration, perseverance, determination, respect and consideration for the opponent, fairness and honesty. These are central to the game and the basis of all other positive attitudes which may be expressed in the game.

I do not think that anyone could dispute the benefits that a commitment to such standards of attitude would have on performance in the game. If you play the game for the right reasons (which, I suggest, is 'for its own sake') then there should be no deviation from these standards. Unfortunately, this ideal is not always followed in practice and some players do play for reasons other than enjoyment and enhancement of quality of life. Many players play for extrinsic reasons which are often the underlying cause of the players' inner negative private feelings and thoughts about the game, and which can result in inappropriate attitudes reflected in their behaviour during the game.

Before looking at the possible causes for an inappropriate attitude and negative thoughts and feelings, it will be helpful to examine what actually occurs in the game, including behaviour in the knock-up period, during and between rallies and at the end of the game. In a way the game can be thought of as a ritual which begins with the pre-contest 'knock-up', continues to the contest, and ends with the shaking of hands when the game is over. How the player behaves during the different phases of the ritual gives us some indication of his attitude.

1. The knock-up period Immediately prior to the game is the time when a player makes his final preparation for the work in that game. The knock-up should be purposeful in that it should be used to familiarise yourself with the hall conditions, i.e. lighting, temperature and shuttle speed, space above and so on. Hence, care and concentration should be apparent as the player gets himself ready for a good standard of performance from the first serve. A state of physical and mental readiness is essential. As the game is not at the contest level at this stage, and the opponent is also preparing himself, some consideration must also be given to his interests. You cannot just use the 'knock-up' period as a means to prepare yourself but must be fair and help your opponent to get ready too, if only to the extent of returning the shuttle to him so that he is able to rally and prepare himself for work. The player who simply hits the shuttle all over the court without regard for the opponent shows a lack of moral concern and certainly lessens the enjoyment of the contest at that stage of the proceedings. Such behaviour could be considered to be in poor taste.

Personally, I believe that much could be done to avoid this situation if there were an accepted form of customary behaviour which all players learnt when they began to play the game. For example, some dignity would be brought to the proceedings if the contest began with the players shaking hands as a formal acknowledgement of each other and the occasion. During the knock-up it should be common practice for players to inform each other what type of stroke-move each wishes to practise. Many young players have no idea how to begin a contest or practise in the knock-up period. It would seem that they do not receive any guidance in this area, and consequently the start of a contest is often vague and lacking in purpose. With guidance, there would be some sort of policy to adopt with the unthinking, insensitive players and even with those intentionally upsetting players who knock-up in a purely selfish way. It would become common practice to insist on receiving a proper knock-up, according to the custom. Indeed, it is most unlikely that once such a custom became an established unwritten rule, any players would break it.

2. The contest Attitudes during the contest can be studied with respect to behaviour during the rally and behaviour between each rally.

a. During the rally

During the rally, an appropriate attitude should be positive with a full commitment to the standards inherent in the game. This is most important in order to make progress in the game. A player should make an honest effort to gain a true measure of his performance; nothing is learnt by holding back. With a full commitment, the player learns about his strengths and weaknesses, i.e. what he can and cannot do; he also learns the same about the opponent, for example, how both behave under pressure when the contest is fiercely fought. You can then do something about what you learn. If a player doesn't make an honest effort, he will never know and always be in doubt about what he can or cannot do. Inevitably, this could lead to defeat in a vital match. So we would expect to see in the player's behaviour signs of care, concentration, determination and so on. Yet even here, some players adopt almost a borderline attitude between what is appropriate and inappropriate with respect to the sort of positive attitude required to win the game. Usually they do so against a weaker opponent and express only a partial commitment to the standards. The result is a performance which for them is mediocre, half-hearted and with attempts to win the rally without too much care and effort, well below their usual standards.

An inappropriate attitude here would be extremely negative, reflecting little commitment to the game. This would be shown in behaviour described as weak, ineffectual, lacking interest, bored and so on. Though here we might be curious why this was so if the player was supposed to be playing the game for his enjoyment. It could be that he was not really in the mood to play or had other things on his mind, but was obliged to take part in this contest. Then perhaps we might show some sympathy for him, for it is something that we all experience at times. Alternatively, it could be that he plays the game for extrinsic reasons and was deliberately not trying for some reason. Then it becomes an entirely different matter and raises problems which will be discussed later (see pages 93–101).

It would seem that there are several possible patterns that attitudes can take during the rally, as shown in the model below.

General attitude		Commitment	Behavioural attitude
Appropriate	positive – up to standard	full	concentration, care, determination, perseverance, fair, sporting etc.
	positive – below standard	partial	half-hearted, lazy, lack of care
Inappropriate	negative – well below standard	none	not trying, no care, thoughtless, aimless, no interest

b. Between the rallies

In between the rallies, players who have shown a negative attitude during the rally will continue in the same vein unless they are deliberately trying to deceive others and also, perhaps, themselves – for example, when a player doesn't bother at all during a rally and is totally negative and then puts on an act that it is all a big joke and fools around in between the rallies. This type of player is a special problem. At this point, however, it is more useful to us to assume that the result is still important to the player and that he wants to win. Behaviour between rallies varies according to whether or not the player is winning or losing. Positive behaviour can occur when the player is winning or losing. Negative behaviour usually occurs only when the player is losing.

An appropriate attitude is positive in two ways. These are:

1. Active purposeful, which is shown in such general behavioural attitudes as brash, cocky, joking, noisy, chatty, bouncy and exuding confidence. These all reflect a player of an extrovert nature.

2. Passive purposeful, which is seen in the player who is calm, quiet, non-commital, serious and unresponsive. This is usually the player of an introvert nature.

An inappropriate attitude would be reflected in negative behaviour of a destructive type in that it can completely destroy the performance and enjoyment of the game as a game in sport. This also takes two forms:

1. Active destructive of an extrovert nature reflected in rudeness, abuse, anger, shouting and arguing, racket throwing, time wasting etc. You can be certain this player cares about winning though he has certainly lost control of how he goes about it. This behaviour should be distinguished from the solitary outburst which is not directed at anyone in particular and can help rather than damage a player's performance. Sometimes the odd outburst can motivate one to try hard.

In active destructive behaviour, the player usually over-steps the moral boundaries, so acting in poor taste and bringing both himself and the game into disrepute. There does exist the odd player who sometimes manages to ride the fine line between comedy and poor taste in his behaviour.

Here there is always the possibility that such behaviour could become 'active purposeful' whilst it is still outgoing and of an extrovert nature. This cannot be said of:

2. Negative destructive behaviour of an inward nature which is to be seen in depression, dejection, misery, lack of confidence, slumping posture, lack of purpose and complete resignation. Once again, such behaviour would indicate a grave concern about winning and for some reason a very negative attitude about the way things are going. Unlike a destructive attitude of the positive type it is most unlikely that the player can get out of this state of mind. Usually it worsens and he is only released from

it with the inevitable defeat. This can be shown more clearly in the diagram below.

Attitude between rallies		*Behaviour*
Positive	active purposeful	confident, bouncy, brash, joking, cocky
	passive purposeful	calm, quiet, serious, non-committal
Negative	active destructive	racket throwing, rude, angry, abusive
	passive destructive	dejected, miserable, sad, resigned, no confidence

These two models simply classify categories of behaviour expressive of the attitudes of different players at different times in the game. They should enable you to identify the behaviour of different players and provide some further insight about what actually goes on in the game and what sort of attitude is most desirable with respect to successful performance and enjoyment.

Attitude at the end of the contest

No matter how the contest was played, at the end one player will have won and the other lost. How does one behave as the victor? This is difficult to say, particularly if the opponent has adopted a negative, active destructive attitude in between rallies. Perhaps it should end just as it began, with a handshake as a formal acknowledgement of the other player and signifying that the contest is at an end. Indeed, this is the normal custom but it would seem that many young players are not fully aware of the point of the custom and allow the handshake to reflect their negative attitude. A weak handshake or a brushing of hands as they go through the motions hardly indicates a genuine acknowledgement of the opponent and an appreciation of the game. At the least, there should be a neutral firm handshake.

Does one do more? Are comments called for on this occasion? I would suggest that custom should require that a quiet 'congratulations' to the winner after a hard fought game would be in the right spirit. One loses little by commenting, 'Well played' or 'Well done' to the winner and from the winner, a return comment or a thanks for the game. It makes the game that much more meaningful and worthwhile, and enhances the quality of the occasion.

The point here is that some conventional customary behaviour is a necessary part of the game, for it places it firmly in a social context, played for the enjoyment of all. It is important that the game is made significant and worthwhile in this respect to indicate that all players actually do show that they care about this game. The attitude of care can only be shown by the way we behave as we take part in the game. To learn and adopt such social customs will help to promote positive appropriate standards of behaviour during a contest. Young players should be taught and expected to conform to these conventional standards, from the start. I am convinced that it will help them with their attitudes later.

So far I have discussed the complexity of attitude with examples of experience and behaviour that are appropriate or inappropriate to the game. The list of appropriate attitudes which derive from the logical nature of the game are central to the game and provide the basis for other appropriate attitudes. For example, 'determination' provides the basis for 'adventurousness'. Only if a player is determined to win will he be prepared to be adventurous. Similarly, 'care' and 'perseverance' provide the basis for 'patience', for only if the player is prepared to maintain his effort over time and take care about how he does things can he be described as patient. Most of the positive attitudes shown by a player are interrelated and connected with these basic ones. Most players do adopt such attitudes in their play, but I think that this is because most players play for the intrinsic enjoyment of the game. They will try hard to win, for they accept that that is the point of the game, but do so knowing that nothing hangs upon the result, or ignoring anything that does. There is also the fact that, if they are keen to improve, they will learn from the experience and then try to eliminate weaknesses from their game.

Furthermore, because they do not think about the outcome, and can concentrate solely on how to defeat the opponent, they become absorbed and lost in a moment. Times seems to stand still for as they concentrate in that moment there is no future and no past. And in this respect the fundamental value of games and sport for man is realised. The activity becomes purely recreational and therapeutic, away from the stress of work. It is pure play and man is better for it.

Inappropriate attitudes: examples, cause, prevention, cure

There are many players who adopt attitudes which are inappropriate in certain respects. In these cases I believe that it is because they also play the game for extrinsic reasons; consequently, a lot hangs upon the result, and winning becomes an important issue. This can cause problems and result in forms of behaviour which are not only socially and morally undesirable but detrimental to performance. It is important to understand this problem to prevent such attitudes from forming, and to alter them if already formed. One way is to consider for what reasons a player might take part in the game, if not for its own sake. To what end is the game a means? And how can such ends cause him to adopt an attitude which is inappropriate in the game?

The answer lies in how the player 'sees' the result with respect to its consequences, and how he assesses the events that occur during play with respect to how they affect the result. So let us try to imagine how a player who uses the game as a means to some end actually 'sees' it. In most cases the 'end' will depend on his success in the game. He must win. There is one exception to this, seen in the player who doesn't want to win because it brings with it further expectations and responsibilities and demands on him. Such a player could actually experience fear at the possibility of winning which might be shown in negative destructive behaviour, dejection etc. There are numerous 'ends' to which success in the game can be a 'means'. These vary in several respects. For example, young teenage tournament players will have different ends to the senior tournament player who wants to become a professional, and both will differ from the professional player.

It would seem a simple matter to ask such players to what extrinsic 'ends' they see the games as a 'means'. We might expect the professional to answer that he sees the game as his work and means of livelihood, and from his success he can earn prize money as well as obtain large contracts from his sponsor; all this enables him to raise his standard of living for himself and his family. In addition he enjoys the social prestige and status that such success brings. It is important to him that he is able to perform well in competition and that nothing, therefore, should happen that is beyond his control, and will affect his chances of winning, e.g. poor court conditions, bad line calls, unfair behaviour from the opponent or a poorly organised tournament.

The tournament player might say that he wants to get into the national team so that he can travel, develop his game and gain some of the 'perks' of top-class players, or become a professional.

The young player may play because he gets the chance to travel, or meet friends and have a good social life, get a break from school, relieve the boredom in holidays and evenings (it's something to do), and it makes him a somebody with his friends and the other kids at school. It is important to be good at something. Finally, as I have suggested, all types of player might genuinely say that fundamentally they play the game because they enjoy it. If this were so, there would be no problems, for although, ideally, it would be good if everyone played solely for the intrinsic value, in practice this is not always the case. You start to play that way but with success there come side benefits which are not always directly related to the game. These are the different 'ends' that success can bring. But as long as the game itself retains its importance and is still the main reason for playing, then the standards within the game will be maintained and performance unaffected by inappropriate attitudes.

However, it is all too easy for the 'ends' to become more important than the game and for too much to hang upon winning. In this case, anything which can affect winning can affect the player's attitude. Thus all these players could become very angry with the cheat who, by cheating, denies them their rights. For the cheat is unfair and it is normal human behaviour to become indignant when someone is unfair. Likewise a 'wrong' line call by the opponent or a line judge can affect the result and prevent a player gaining his 'important' ends. So frustration and anger can develop and be directed at the cheat or the line judge.

Such behaviour could be reasonable and justified, and we might consider it appropriate though rather strong. Unfortunately, even justified attitudes may be inappropriate to performance. If a player sees a situation as 'angry-making' because he believes that the cheat or the line judge has been unfair, even though each could have made a genuine judgement, then his attitude could cause him to lose concentration and may affect his standard of performance. That is why the player who cheats deliberately, to provoke such an attitude, is particularly distasteful in the game. Players must be on their guard that one attitude does not spark off another one which is detrimental to good performance. Some degree of control can be maintained just as long as the 'ends' do not become more important than the 'means' (the game itself). Then a player can resort to the rules of the game for guidance and remain firmly objective with the cheat or the 'unfair' line call. There are procedures that can be followed to cover most incidents that occur in the game in this respect. Once again it is important that all players are taught from the beginning how to apply the rules of the game in games with or without officials, i.e. what rule applies and what to say, to whom to say it and how to say it.

In fact those players now committed to professionalism in the game do give a sound performance on most occasions. The game is their craft and if they want to master their craft and succeed in it they have little alternative but to adopt the right attitude. Competition is so strong that they must either conform to the standards or fail. Those that do fail may either lack the discipline to conform to do the work necessary to reach high standards of technical/tactical and physical competence, or fail because they are unable, for some reason, to adopt an appropriate attitude to the game.

In general, it is not the player who consciously enjoys the game, both as a game and as a means to other ends, who is affected seriously by attitude problems. Such players are conscious of why they play and thus can be realistic about it and maintain some degree of control over how they play and behave in the game. Nor does attitude affect the player who plays solely for extrinsic ends, for in his case anything goes so long as he wins. He might be extremely fair and maintain all the standards appropriate to the game but he plays cold-bloodedly for the benefits success brings. There need be no enjoyment in the game for him: he must simply produce an efficient piece of work. Alternatively, he might cheat, bend the rules, upset people and devise all sorts of tactics to gain his success and the benefits that he wants from the game. Such players can act intentionally, either within or outside the boundaries of what is appropriate to the game. It doesn't really matter either way to them, for the game doesn't really matter. All that matters are the ends the game can be used to bring about.

The serious problem lies with the player who is not consciously aware, or won't admit, that he plays either for or to avoid those extrinsic ends which affect his self-image. It is this problem I shall now consider.

Attitude and the self-image

Winning or losing has important consequences for the type of player we have been discussing, with respect to his self-image. I would suggest that even though such players may play for specific objectives, failure does not simply result in disappointment at not reaching the objective but results in damage to the self-image. And the threat of that occurring once the player begins a contest can cause a very negative attitude.

Even the successful player who doesn't want to win because of the responsibility and success it brings, feels this way because that much more will be expected from him and so greater will be the damage to his self-image when he does fail to win. It is quite true in this sense that 'the bigger they come the harder they fall' and such a player may try to avoid the hard fall by trying to avoid getting bigger. In fact he is in a predicament, for he cannot avoid playing unless he gives up the game, which for some reason he is unable to do. So he must continually face up to the possibility of getting bigger in status and prestige and with it the increasing fear of failure. The more successful he is, the greater will appear the risk he takes each time he steps onto the court. And should he fail, greater will be the damage, in his eyes, to his self-image.

I think that problems of self-image happen today particularly with young players, even though I have known experienced internationals to feel fear on the court at the thought of losing. Consider the example of the player who is expected to win against an inferior opponent and who, having lost the first set, is 11–8 up in the second. Suddenly, he begins to snatch at his strokes, plays tentatively, doesn't recover to cover the replies quickly enough and so loses the match. He has suffered, apparently, from 'nerves' and his performance has been affected. One possible reason is that he had doubts and thought he might lose. What would the consequences of losing be? To lose to such a player when everyone expects him to win; what would others think of him, and what a fool or failure he would appear to his fellow players. This is something he couldn't cope with. He 'sees' the result as having social consequences affecting his status in the eyes of others, and with it the damage he would experience to his self-image. So he experiences the emotion of fear and his behaviour on the court is affected. He tenses up and fails to perform with his normal expertise.

Another example is the player who adopts the wrong attitude before or during the game, not solely because he might lose but because he believes he will lose. Losing will have disastrous consequences for his self-image and social status. So he doesn't bother to try to win and instead attempts ridiculous shots, makes appeals to the heavens and fools around, all with a 'couldn't care less' attitude. When he does lose he has his excuses ready and avoids the harm to his image. Wasn't it obvious to all that he hadn't tried and how can you be said to have failed unless you have tried? He has separated losing from failing as a person, for he can always argue that if he had really tried then he would have won. But to try to win he would have had to commit himself fully to the task and that would have required an honest effort which would have exposed him to the critical eyes of others. And as he believes that failure in the game is synonymous with failure as a person, losing becomes a blow to his self-esteem. The consequences of losing are too important to risk an honest performance. In trying to deceive his audience he deceives only himself.

The pressure of expectations

The expectations of other people, e.g. parents, friends, other players, coaches and officials, can have a disastrous effect on some players. In this respect young players are particularly vulnerable. In sport in general, and in badminton in particular, there is a tremendous promotion of youth participation in organised competition. The desire to promote badminton among the young also includes the desire to produce champions. Nowadays, we have organised tournament play and squad systems from the under tens upwards. Children are coached, selected for squad training and then pushed into tournament play and competitive match play at all levels (including national level). They are expected to attend training and practice sessions or else their interest is questioned. Proud, well-intentioned parents, coaches and officials now take a ride 'on the backs of children', bask in their success and feel dismayed if they lose. The adult lives through the child and the child has to meet the adult's expectations. The pressures are on the children to do well. The ten- and twelve-year olds compare notes about whom one should expect to beat and not to beat; for haven't the knowledgeable adults made their authoritative judgements, and aren't John and Mary being coached by Mr Goldracket and hasn't the county official selected them for the team. They *must* be good! How can either be beaten or not expect to win? Neither can they be expected to lose against someone who is an unheard-of nobody.

So here we are on court.
"I can't lose against her. She's a nobody and everyone expects me to beat her. But what if I should lose?"
"How could you lose to her? Look at all the work you have done and all the

coaching and training you have had. Why didn't you try? What went wrong? Fancy losing to her!"

"How can I be winning against him? He is a somebody. He has won this and that and is seeded and plays for the region and the schools side and everyone knows he is good. I'm just a nobody and I can't beat a somebody. He is going to start trying in a minute and then I can't win."
"Well, you gave him a good run. A pity you couldn't keep it up. Better luck next time!"

I know of two young players who had the misfortune to be talented in towns where the adults organising the game had forgotten that the game is for the enjoyment of the individuals who play it. One, a natural games player, suddenly found that some success had led to his whole season being completely organised for him, including when he had his days off. Furthermore, he was expected to comply with this programme if he wanted to be selected for the county junior team. Selection on merit was suddenly forgotten and a condition of any further play had to be his complete conformity to the system. Fortunately, he was a sensible lad and had non-interfering parents. He got out quickly and returned to play his beloved football which he had risked losing in order to attend the 'voluntary' Saturday morning badminton squad sessions. He was fourteen years old.

The other, a girl, was expected to attend all sorts of organised commitments and was severely criticised and subjected to threats about her future in the game if she did not attend. When she looked unhappy at sessions or spoke up she was castigated for her bad attitude and made to feel that she was ungrateful for everything that was being done for her and the time that others were putting in on her behalf. After suffering a completely miserable period on the court and many sleepless nights which resulted in being prescribed sleeping pills and tranquillisers from her doctor, she was advised to withdraw from the various squads. This she did with support from her parents, and officials with imagination and the right values in the game. She began to play the game for herself again rather than for the ambitious, demanding organisers, and recovered her health and her enjoyment of the game. She was sixteen.

It is unfortunate that too many well-intentioned adults have organised the game at too insistent a level for many young players. As a result, there are many sensitive young adolescent players who suffer unnecessarily and opt out as soon as they can. It is one thing to organise badminton for young players and encourage them in their play. It is another to place too much pressure on youngsters with unrealistic expectations whilst they are still learning and improving their performance in the game. Children have many interests and pressures which arise from school. The game is for their recreation and enjoyment from organised competition. Not everyone wants to or will become a champion, even though at that time he or she may be the greatest junior player the world has ever seen. Those who want to become champions at the adult level may do so in spite of the system and suddenly appear from nowhere.

Too many expectations can be placed upon the youngsters; and when results become all-important and the emphasis isn't on whether the young player enjoys the game or is developing certain aspects of skill, but whether or not he or she wins, then there is a danger of causing psychological damage. Prestige and social status, attention and respect from friends and players, officials, coaches and parents are often gained by successful performance. Winners become somebodies. They get spoken to and watched when they play. Success is everything and standards of performance in skill and attitude are allowed to fall as long as the player is the winner.

Children suffer in this syndrome, for they are still acquiring beliefs and values about their social reality and what is and is not important in it. To make winning more important than it is and to equate success in a game with value as a person in a social group, is to teach the wrong values and to present an undesirable picture of reality. In fact, the idea of wanting to win because it makes one important is really totally irrelevant to the game. It may motivate you to try harder sometimes and initially foster interest in the game, but it can just as easily cause the opposite effect and result in the unnecessary suffering of the young player.

I have deliberately discussed the problem of the young player, mainly to draw attention to a matter of grave concern in the development of players in the game. The promotion of appropriate attitudes comes from encouraging players in general, and children in particular, to play the game for its own sake. By all means let the authorities organise formal competition for young players; trying to win is the point of the game and provides the challenge and the enjoyment – but do not create a situation in which self-image and social status hang upon the result. It cannot be totally avoided, but its importance can be considerably reduced by emphasising those features of the game which genuinely matter – those features that you experience by playing the game for its own sake. The benefit of such emphasis is to see players who are free from fear and able to commit themselves fully to attaining a good level of performance and success in the game.

The value of this discussion is that it draws attention to why players behave in different ways. What we learn from it is that we must know something about the players' beliefs and values to understand their attitudes. My concern has been mainly with the negative inner experiences and inappropriate attitudes, for they are the type that badly affect the standards of performance. What I have said about children also applies to adults. It is most likely that what many suffer as adults is because of how they experienced the game as children. We can prevent the development of inappropriate attitudes in children in the way we teach and organise the game for them, by being realistic about children's badminton and teaching them to play the game for its own sake. There will, of course, still be some who give up the game as other interests take priority; others will continue in clubs and some will become champions and professional players. But perhaps all will do so with an attitude that reflects a positive inner experience of the game as one which has been worthwhile and rewarding.

There still remains the problem of those players who do possess a negative attitude to the game. What can we do about them? It would seem that if certain beliefs and values cause inner experiences which result in particular attitudes, then we must examine those beliefs and values and assess their validity. For example, do other people really think that you are a failure as a person in some way if you fail to win? Are you really stupid if you make a silly shot? I very much doubt that the facts support the player's beliefs about what he thinks others think about his performance.

Should a player go on court and expect to win? Yes, if it is Rudi Hartono playing a beginner. He would be silly not to. But if it is two equal opponents or an unknown opponent, then one has to wait and see. The same applies about going on court and expecting to lose. You cannot, unless you know that the gap between you and the other player is very wide, i.e. you know that you both play on entirely different levels and you can make a realistic assessment of your standards. But when the gap is unknown or known to be close then you cannot predict the outcome. It is unrealistic to do so. That would be more a sign of stupidity than anything else. Those people – parents, coaches, officials, friends and the like – who predict the outcome prior to a game simply place an unwanted extra burden on the player. It is called 'the pressure of expectations'. And if placed on those players who are subject to an inappropriate attitude, then it will certainly cause one. Comments about the possible result will not affect the supremely confident player who has a full commitment to the game, for it is most unlikely that such a player will take much notice. He will have made his own assessment of the contest and isn't dependent on others for the attitude he adopts. It is a pity that the problem ever arises, for there is enough to work on in the game without getting involved with the status of 'self'. I am sure that many youngsters would not do so if they were not pressurised by unrealistic adult expectations and beliefs about the value of success. Young players brought up with an objective approach to the game would learn to be objective in their appraisals and realistic about winning and losing. If they could place the result in perspective then, as adults, they would not suffer the results of inappropriate attitudes developed in their formative years. It would certainly result in a richer game for all.

One way to ensure this and prevent or cure the problem is to encourage players to think critically: to question the comments and statements of coaches and others; to ask, 'How do they know?' and 'Are they right?'; to examine the facts and make a realistic assessment of their chances in a game. To do this it is necessary to learn about the game and what counts as 'good' in the game with regard to the standards of skill and fitness and the attitude appropriate to it. And finally, just make sure that in learning the game, you play for the right reasons – the game itself.

By looking at things in this way players may find that they hold irrational beliefs and the wrong values. However, if they are able to change their beliefs and values in the light of the facts, they should come to 'see' the game differently. They will have different experiences and attitudes in the game. You can change your attitude by changing your beliefs and your values. There is the odd exception, when a player accepts that his beliefs are invalid and yet continues to see the game in the same way. He knows that he is wrong but just cannot change his emotional response to the result and its consequences. In such a case it is sometimes possible to overcome an inappropriate attitude with a stronger appropriate attitude. For example, fear can be overcome by courage and doubt by determination. In such instances the player requires 'character' and the 'will' to overcome his feelings and adopt attitudes more appropriate to successful performance.

Discipline in performance

It is often a matter of some debate whether all players possess sufficient character and the ability to control feelings with stronger attitudes. Some would argue that character and strength of will are inherited – you either have such qualities or you don't. I would doubt this and argue that they are qualities that are developed in and through the work people do and are achieved by discipline. This conveys the idea of submission to rules or some kind of order. In badminton, the discipline is to submit yourself to the work required to attain the standards of excellence within the different aspects of performance. The attitudes adopted in work are most important, for the work demands some degree of sacrifice to attain skill and fitness. At the highest levels the player must submit himself to practice and much physical work. Practice entails continuous work on the technical/tactical aspects of skill to achieve control and accuracy at speed in the tactical situations in the game. Anything detrimental to achieving that standard is ruled out. A player cannot miss his practice; he must make time and sacrifice his other interests to do it. Similarly with fitness, which involves a balance of training, diet and rest. The highest standard is his potential maximum fitness. The rigours of training required to reach this standard rule out anything detrimental to it. Players who do not maintain regular training sessions; who do not work hard in training; who overeat, smoke or drink too much alcohol, and fail to get their necessary sleep, will find it difficult to attain the standard. The penalty for any neglect is a lower standard of fitness and consequently a lower standard of performance in the game. The responsibility for attaining these standards rests with the player. If he wants to do well he must submit himself to the standards required. Those that do so, naturally acquire the discipline to maintain them in competition and thus adopt appropriate attitudes. Too much work has been done and too many sacrifices made not to use these attitudes when the chance to perform arises. Through the work the player has learned to lift himself when tired or bored and frustrated. In preparation, he has overloaded the work to ensure that there is nothing in the game that he cannot contend with. The disciplined player is trained like the good actor. No matter how tired, upset or fearful he feels, 'the show must go on', and accordingly he submits himself to the discipline of his craft and gives a good performance. In this way the years of training and sacrifice, in striving for standards, pay off.

Attitudes and experiences in training

Even though discipline develops in the work and from doing the work to learn the craft, this doesn't imply that a player *must* suffer pain and hardship in training, particularly in the areas which require much physical work. Technical and fitness standards can be attained with a minimum of hardship if they are approached with the right sort of attitude. There are different approaches to physical work, particularly in fitness training.

This can be seen as a demanding, challenging business requiring hard slog, sweat, and punishing yourself as you push through the mythical 'pain barrier'. Here it is seen as necessary to *suffer* the experience as though this was the only evidence that you had worked hard. So the athlete is motivated to work and drive himself to the point of exhaustion in the belief that he has only worked hard if he has reached such a state. Such an approach may achieve the desired physical results but is amazingly crude and negative in its approach. Training here is seen as something one suffers and endures rather than as an experience that one can enjoy and look forward to. In training, a player must work in accordance with the principle of overload and progression simply to achieve a training effect and get fitter (see page 83). Yet it doesn't follow that he must add the principle of 'suffering' to prove that he has overloaded his body to make progress. In fact the training experience can be enjoyable and rewarding if you approach it with a different attitude.

An approach to training

In training you should get to know your body and 'inside' it to some extent. Then you experience your body as a total unified organism with all the parts operating in harmony. In most forms of exercising, particularly running, rhythm is an essential factor in experiencing the joy of exercise. For example, when running, it is possible to concentrate on the rhythm of breathing and the step pattern until both are synchronised and one begins to get lost in the rhythm. Here, good technique in terms of carriage, posture and balance as the trunk settles on the legs, with relaxed loose arms swinging freely from the shoulders without strain, and easy light steps, all contribute to easy rhythmic running. Running is then effortless and involves tension without strain. In this way you become free from your body. But, if there is strain and unnecessary tension caused by poor technique, your body is in internal conflict and struggling to do the work, and this is very noticeable.

Children possess this freedom, for they run with feet which fly across the ground 'defying' gravity. Man naturally possesses a quality of movement but loses it unless he persists with his running from childhood and continues to enjoy the experience. With good technique and rhythm it is possible to become lost in the rhythm. As one gets 'inside' the body, it is but a small step to get 'outside' the body and free from it. Then you run with a quality akin to floating – completely effortless. Here there is work without strain and the experience is totally enjoyable. When the body is in harmony then you forget it. It seems not to exist and you become free to focus thought on other matters beyond the self or achieve a state of no thought. Time now stands still, for you become part of the moment and absorbed in the experience. Much depends on the strength of the body and its capacity to diminish hard work. It is difficult to achieve this state unless the body is fit. And to achieve fitness does not require punishing training sessions.

There is a technique which requires the application of a particular attitude towards physical work in training and practice. It is not only applicable to running but to all forms of exercise, requiring an act of concentration which involves conscious thought or a process of conscious 'no thought'. An example will make this clear. Sometimes you receive an injury which results in a nagging, throbbing pain. It hurts. If you fight the pain it tends to hurt even more and can cause you to grit your teeth to bear the pain. This is what happens when you suffer pain in training from hard exercise. You fight harder to overcome it and it hurts even more; so more fight is called for. The fact that the injury nags and throbs would indicate that it has its own rhythm. To lose the pain is quite easy, for the answer is to concentrate on the rhythm of the pain. Instead of experiencing the pain as something foreign to the body you accept it totally and concentrate on it. You become the pain by getting into the rhythm of the pain. As you do so the pain disappears. That is one way.

Another way is not to consciously think about the pain; to think about something else or to think nothing, an act of meditation which results in your 'leaving' the body, for in meditating you lose conscious awareness of it. You step outside your own body and in so doing the physical pain disappears along with the body. This technique can be used to develop a similar sort of attitude to body training, e.g. press-ups and sit-ups. You simply concentrate on the rhythm of the exercise and lose yourself in the rhythm. The body then works without strain and in complete harmony and you enjoy your body working; very much conscious of it but unaffected by it. A simple case of this is something most players experience when they are skipping in training.

Skip without music and the work can be quite tedious. Skip with pop music, concentrate on the rhythm, and the skipping becomes effortless and the work without strain. Of course with concentration you could also skip without music and immerse yourself in the rhythm of the body movement to achieve the same effect.

This doesn't mean, however, that you can go on indefinitely. The body is a chemical organism and work will use up the fuel which produces the energy and produce waste deposits which build up in the muscles. When the energy supply has been used up completely or when too much waste deposit has built up then the muscles will cease to function. The work stops, either to remove waste deposits or take in more fuel. During that period you must rest. However, this doesn't alter the point that even severe training, relative to the fitness of the athlete, can be enjoyable as an experience in which one can lose itself in the activity.

If this state is achieved in competition then you can lose yourself and be free to focus attention on the opponent totally. Your body functions as the instrument through which you express your thoughts intuitively in the stroke-moves you use to defeat your opponent.

Attitude in competition

I have discussed at length what counts as an appropriate attitude in competition by analysing the game to sort out those attitudes fundamental to it. The competition is the test of attitude. However, when the contest is a close one and skill, fitness and attitude are equal then a player must call on something extra. In some way he must intensify his efforts. This is where the discipline developed in preparation gains its rewards. For through the work the player has disciplined himself to attain the high standards necessary to performance and thus knows that he is capable of performing well. He knows that he is up to the task. Inevitably this will result in confidence in his own ability. In this way doubts are prevented or removed and he can concentrate on the task of winning. But something more is needed, if all things are equal. That is character and the will to win which, though it comes through and from the work, is also unique to each individual. It is the combination of mental toughness and spirit that enables a player to intensify his resolution and lift himself to that extra dimension of human endeavour. He raises his standards. Thus we see, and the opponent feels, that total commitment, cold determination, absolute concentration, rigid control, continual perseverance, complete care and adventurousness as chances are taken fearlessly. Now that player is totally lost in the moment in single-minded pursuit of his victory and under such relentless pressure the opponent must eventually succumb.

Even this ability can be helped to emerge, although it is something unique to an individual. In practice and training it is possible to set very high standards of performance. A player, therefore, could develop a level of technical skill and fitness which is far higher than any other player's. Then his 'basic standard' performance would be equal to any other player's highest standard. Consequently, if another player managed to raise his standard of performance in a contest, our player could simply raise his beyond his basic standard. In this way he appears to play at a much higher level than anyone else.

To achieve this in practice and training requires a total commitment to the work and a very disciplined attitude. Attitude is developed to high levels along with the skill and fitness. Such a player does not see his attitude and level of performance as being anything special and on court it takes little extra effort to behave in such a way. Only to the opponent and the spectators does he appear to be superhuman.

Another way this can be achieved is to take a particular approach to the importance of certain events in the game. For example, if the player has trained to perform at very high standards and considers this to be quite normal then for him there will be nothing special about what he considers to be normal things. He would kill a shuttle from just above net height as a routine matter, not as the adventurous risky move most players would judge it to be. And because each stroke-move had a purpose there would be nothing special about a winning smash. It would be no more special than the 'clear' three moves back which created the situation for the smash. In such play there are no highlights. Everything is of equal importance. If this was not so then the winning smash could cause a lapse in concentration and sense of purpose. There may be inner excitement or satisfaction at that stage of the contest and he may inwardly rest on his laurels and relax for a moment. But, if no one move is more special or important than any other, then all require equal concentration and commitment and care in their execution. At this point, the player cannot even share the applause of the audience when they see the kill as a highlight, for to him it is quite normal and there is much hard work to be done. Only when the contest is over can he enjoy his victory for a short period before he prepares for the next match.

The player, in his act of concentration, can still be adventurous in taking his chances, but this is to be expected, for adventurousness is only an expression of his concentration and intuition. If his concentration lapses, then the intuition that there is a chance to make a move may result in action that fails to achieve its purpose.

To play in this way demands a greater sense of purpose from the player. He must be clear about the outcome once he steps onto the court, and then work single-mindedly towards achieving it. As nothing is special and there is no relaxation until the job is completed then the player works calmly towards that end. And if he can achieve this state of calm, undisturbed by irrelevant emotions and unnecessary passion he should perform well and enhance his chances of success.

The exploitation of attitude

If attitude is a part of performance then one could argue that it is a fair target for tactical exploitation. Just as we try to find weaknesses in the opponent's skill and fitness then we should also try to find weaknesses in his attitude.

This is the area where gamesmanship arises. The danger is that one can go too far and overstep the moral boundaries which underpin the rules of the game. The principles of fairness, respect and consideration for the opponent still apply. Nevertheless, within these boundaries there is scope to test out the opponent's attitude. You could try to upset his concentration by playing a game which is not in keeping with his style. You could take a player who likes to play a quick game and slow the game down, thus making him impatient and frustrated and, perhaps, force errors. Alternatively, you could play a fast game against a slow player. To upset a player's attitude within the area of tactics and fitness seems right and proper and good strategy. As such you should seriously consider how this can be achieved. It is questionable how far this can be taken in between rallies, for then it is all too easy to go too far. It is acceptable perhaps to 'stare' at the opponent just prior to the serve; to announce the score calmly and deliberately as though you intended to take a complete grip on the game and turn on a special performance. It is acceptable to keep the pressure on by wasting no time between rallies, purposefully picking up the shuttle and getting on with the game. It might be acceptable to take one's time between the rallies as if preparing oneself for a more determined effort (but it would not be acceptable to waste time deliberately, though obviously this is difficult to prove). It would not be acceptable to pause and stop just as the opponent is about ready to serve or to receive. Once or twice for good reason, but not frequently, for then it becomes obvious that the action is deliberately designed to upset the other. Some players try to upset others by talking, making comments and fooling around. Others question line decisions, forget the score or even claim the wrong score, in their favour. When this reaches the stage of deliberate cheating then it must be condemned strongly. What is acceptable is a matter of judgement and opinion in many cases, but in others, there are the laws of the game which stipulate how players should behave, and recommend procedure when these rules are broken. It is up to every player to learn the rules of the game just as he learns the skills of the game, and to formulate his policy when opponents try to exploit his attitude unfairly. Fair attempts should not bother the player who is committed to the job at hand and has adopted an appropriate attitude towards it, for little should disturb him in this respect.

Conclusion

I have discussed attitude in some depth in order to provide some insight into its importance and place in the game. It connects with inner experiences, emotions and feelings and public behaviour on the court. It is a central area in sports psychology simply because it is so complex and yet so essential in the performance of any player. I know that this discussion raises questions which are left unanswered. This should not cause any undue concern, for the sole intention has been to examine attitude, its many facets and its connection with skill and fitness.

Part Three

Playing the Game

Chapter 7 The Three Basic Moves

By now you should possess a clearer picture of the game and appreciate the significance of your skill, fitness and attitude in improving your performance in the game. But you may wonder how you can learn to make the stroke-moves to defeat your opponents. The simple answer is that you learn them by playing them. Give some thought to the use of a stroke as a move – your intention, the effect on your opponent, his possible replies, your recovery and whether the move is in accordance with the principle of attack. If you are not sure or get yourself into difficult situations, refer to the charts for guidance (pages 30–35).

If you are an experienced player, at club or international level, you can begin to do this at any point in the game. Just 'stand back' and reflect on your game in terms of stroke-moves, their replies and your travel between situations. You may find that you do this anyway, although you may not have thought about it in these terms. Some thought may reveal that you are weak in certain situations, and need to learn a few more stroke-moves or work harder on your recovery between moves. If so, use the framework to examine and evaluate your game. Then select your starting point on the charts.

If, however, you are just learning to play or would prefer to have a specific starting point then begin with the three basic moves. Even experienced international players I have coached have benefited from working on the three basic moves. Perhaps this is because all the stroke-moves used in the game can be reduced to these three moves. For example: Fleming Delf's renowned backhand clear is just a move to the rearcourt; the Sidek backhand spin serve was simply (though difficult to reply to) a move to the forecourt; and Liem Swie King's powerful steep smash, that he jumps so high to hit down, is just a move to the midcourt. The different variations on the basic moves simply make them more effective as attacking moves in accordance with the principle of attack.

Learning the basic moves

Let's imagine we are about to play a game of singles and then trace our progress through the game as we examine what arises when we make the basic moves in accordance with the principle of attack. Once the contest begins, your sole aim is to win. Thus, throughout each rally in the game, you should try to create a situation to make a scoring hit. To do this you will use the three basic moves. These are:

1. To hit the shuttle to the rearcourt – over my head or past me down the sides of the court with clears or lobs.
2. To hit the shuttle to the forecourt – with dropshots or net shots.
3. To hit the shuttle downwards to the sides or centre of the midcourt – with a smash.

The basic strokes required to do this are: the high and low serve; the overhead clear, drop and smash; the block, lob and push replies to the smash; and the lob or net replies in the forecourt.

It will help to remind you of the reasons for the basic moves.

1. The hit to the rearcourt makes it difficult for me to make a scoring hit because it places me so far from the net, for obviously, the nearer I am to the net the easier it is to make a winning hit from a high position. Additionally, if I should drop or clear from the rearcourt you will have more time to travel and make your next stroke-move. Finally, it also places me out of position away from my centre and control of the space in the court and, unless I recover quickly after my reply, you might also have created extra space to hit the shuttle into.

    So, if you do intend to play a move to the rearcourt, make sure that you really push me back the full distance. Check my feet to ensure that I hit my reply from within the rearcourt lines. Then you can be certain you have hit a good stroke-move.
2. The hit to the forecourt also places me out of position and creates space if I am slow to recover. In addition it forces me to hit the shuttle upwards, which allows you to threaten with a strong downward hit.
3. The strong downward hit to the midcourt either hits the ground to end the rally or forces a weaker lift for the shuttle to be hit down from nearer the net. Unless, of course, my hitting technique and range of stroke-moves allow me to reply with a lob to your rearcourt. For you must remember that whilst you are making these moves I will be trying to play counter-moves against you.

The opening move – the serve

There are two basic serve-moves. These are: to serve the shuttle high over my head to the rearcourt – the high serve; or to serve the shuttle low over the net towards the forecourt/midcourt area – the low serve. Knowing this, I prepare to guard against the main threat, the serve to the rearcourt. I want to be able to travel quickly to make a smash reply. At the same time, I must take some precautions against the low serve and be prepared to travel forwards to hit the shuttle down from above the net, or play a net reply and try to force

Plate 31.
Receiving serve

you to lift it for me to hit down. So I position myself in the midcourt in a *backward attacking stance*, the best starting position for quick backward travel when I want to protect my rearcourt (see plate 31). The left leg is forwards and the racket held with the head above the hand ready to threaten and hit downwards.

Most probably you will now serve a very high defensive serve deep into the rearcourt to ensure that the shuttle drops vertically, making it more difficult for me to time my smash. Nevertheless, I must travel quickly backwards and get into the 'smash position' (see plate 32). This is the most threatening position I can adopt, for, if I am in balance and able to smash hard, I can force you to adopt a defensive stance (see plate 33) to guard against the main threat – my smash to the sides or centre of your midcourt. To defend, you would stand square on to me facing down the funnel (see page 42), with feet apart ready to step sideways to receive the smash. If, instead, you serve low then you must recover quickly to threaten my reply.

Plate 32 (facing).
The smash position

Plate 33.
Defensive stance

Plate 34.
Forward attacking stance

Here you would usually adopt a *forward attacking stance* ready to attack any replies to your forecourt (see plate 34). To do this you stand with your right foot forwards, racket ready to attack any forecourt reply. This is the main danger in the situation for, if successful, it may force you to lift the shuttle high. By threatening my reply to the forecourt you place extra pressure on me and may force me to lift the shuttle high for you to hit down.

It should by now be obvious that how you stand and hold your racket is very important in any situation in the game. And as the basic stances are linked to the basic moves it becomes possible to suggest some general rules for you to follow.

Plate 35. The attack position

1. The backward attacking stance is used when you decide the main threat is the hit to the rearcourt.
2. The forward attacking stance is used when you decide the main threat is the hit to the forecourt.
3. The defensive stance is used when the main threat is the smash to the midcourt.
4. The smash position is taken up to enable you to threaten to hit down from the rearcourt or midcourt and so force your opponent to use a defensive stance.
5. The racket is held ready to threaten to attack at all times.

I often think of the racket as a weapon held ready to deliver a blow to the opponent or defend against a blow by counter-hitting. Consequently, like a weapon, it should be held in front of the body with the racket head pointing upwards, indicating that the 'weapon' hand is alert and ready to hit. This is the 'attack position' seen in the attacking and defensive stances (see plate 35).

The basic moves played after the serve

1. The high serve

After your high serve I would travel back quickly and take up the smash position. In this situation I can smash to the midcourt (the main threat which you must guard against), clear to your rearcourt or drop to your forecourt. If I clear to your rearcourt you can use the same three basic moves against me, and so I must travel to the midcourt to take up a defensive stance. If I drop to your forecourt I must travel forwards to take up a forward or backward attacking stance, depending on whether you look as if to reply with moves to the forecourt or rearcourt. If I smash I will travel forwards ready to threaten your reply to the forecourt, midcourt or rearcourt.

2. The low serve

If I reply with a move to the forecourt, I would take up the forward or backward attacking stance according to which stroke-move I expect from you. Should I clear to the rearcourt, I would usually take up a defensive stance, unless I manage to get the shuttle past you and expect you to make a weak reply.

The game is one in which we continually use the basic moves against each other and take up stances which enable us to attack or defend against them. If we are both very fit and get into position quickly to make stroke-moves, the game could go on indefinitely. Fortunately it doesn't, for players have used their intelligence and imagination to develop the game beyond this level and made it a battle of minds.

Making effective stroke-moves

My problem is how to ensure that my stroke-move is effective and gets the sort of reply I want from you. For example:

How can I prevent you from getting into the smash position to threaten me from the rearcourt and, instead, force you to give me a weak reply?

How can I ensure that you are late arriving into the forecourt and will give a weak lift that I can hit down?

How can I ensure that if I smash to your midcourt you will block to my forecourt and give me a chance to hit down, or force you to make a weak lift towards the rearcourt?

Even if I cannot ensure that I get the replies I want, I must try to create situations which might obtain those replies and increase my chances of winning. And whatever I do, you will also be trying to make stroke-moves to obtain the replies you want to increase your chances of winning. In this way the game becomes a battle of wits as we both try to make stroke-moves which create situations to our advantage. By mastering our hitting and travelling techniques on the court, we can become free from physical incompetence to concentrate solely on the task of outwitting each other. This can be done as follows.

Let's begin in the rearcourt and assume that I am poised in the smash position. It is most important that you know I can hit a power smash for then you are more or less forced to take up a defensive stance. If you fail to do so, there is more possibility that I will use my smash with greater effect – and I assume you wouldn't want that to happen. However, once you do adopt a defensive stance you are set in position until I actually hit the shuttle, and I can 'keep' you there as long as my racket preparation looks the same for all my overhead stroke-moves. Now, perhaps, I can make a surprise move, such as an attack clear to your rearcourt, or a check-smash or sliced dropshot to your forecourt. The direction in which I hit the shuttle depends on what replies you might make or which side is the weaker, but the main effect of my 'smash position' is to make you wait and consequently late in travelling to the rearcourt or forecourt. I know that you will usually reach the shuttle, but too late to threaten me from the rearcourt and do anything but lift from the forecourt. In fact I may even obtain a weak reply or catch you out completely and win the rally. If I do use the smash-move then I will hang back in the rearcourt, leaving you plenty of court space, and 'invite' you to make the block return to the forecourt. I know that if I rush forwards after my smash you could flick the shuttle over my head and catch me out, so preventing me from making another power smash and even forcing a weak reply for you to attack. So I hang back. Now we have another little battle in the new situation. I realise that you might block the smash and try to get the shuttle below net level before I arrive to hit it. If you do so you will usually take up a forward attacking stance, threaten my forecourt reply and try to force me to lift. So, to prevent this, I approach the forecourt with my racket head up in the 'attack position', threatening to hit down. This action usually has the effect of making you pause and remain in the midcourt to guard against my possible downward hit. I will now have created some space and even if I cannot hit down at least I will be able to play an effective 'tumbler' without fear. The danger is that if you are quick and see me lower my racket head to play a net reply, you will begin to travel forwards. To prevent you doing this again, or to catch you out, I could whip the shuttle, from near the top of the net, past you or above you to the rearcourt. Next time you might not be so eager to anticipate my stroke-move.

In this way the game progresses to a higher level and the emphasis switches to the effectiveness of a stroke-move in achieving its objective. One way to assure this is to make you, as my opponent, delay your preparation and travel to hit the shuttle in each new situation. This I would try to achieve by looking as if to play my strongest threat in each situation. In the rearcourt I would take up the smash position whenever possible. In the forecourt, I would look as if to hit down to keep you away from the net, or to make a forecourt move to bring you forwards so that I could flick the shuttle over your head to the rearcourt. In fact, our battle of wits now includes the use of strokes, not only to make moves but to deceive each other as we do so.

Deception

Among the many attractions of badminton are the numerous opportunities that occur for deceiving your opponent. There is much pleasure in keeping the opponent guessing and then tempting him to go the wrong way for the shuttle. I was fortunate enough to see in the 1960s Finn Kobbero, whose skill was so great that even his fellow players would crowd around the court to see what new trick he pulled out of the bag.

To some extent the art of deception has been neglected in the modern game of badminton. During the 1970s, there was much emphasis on speed and fitness, which reduced the need for deception. Additionally, there has been an increase in the amount of coaching, which has resulted in many players learning strokes and practising routines with mechanical efficiency. Deception seems to have been ignored, for it is not something concrete, like a stroke, that can be abstracted from the game and practised in isolation. It is an elusive quality that only makes sense when related to an opponent. Without an opponent there can be no deception. Perhaps this is one reason why players of earlier days used more deception, for they taught themselves through actual playing and their focus was always on the opponent and not on stroke production. Now that things have equalled out and the majority of players are very fit and skilful, there is once again a need for more deception to tip the balance between winning and losing.

Deception takes the form of a pretence by a player, who tries to communicate to his opponent his intention to do one thing, by looking as if to make a specific move, when in actual fact he intends to make another move. For example, I could pretend to smash and then hit an attack clear. I could intend to deceive you in all sorts of ways but I will not know you have been deceived until you make the response I want you to. So when I pretend to smash, and you recognise my behaviour as 'he looks as if to smash behaviour', you will make the 'correct' response and take up the defensive stance. I could now hit the shuttle over your head and succeed in deceiving you.

As I communicate my intention to smash through my movements it is important to me that I know you will recognise those movements as 'looking to smash behaviour'. Otherwise my deception will not succeed. I must present a picture of myself which you see and interpret as being of a certain sort. Your response indicates your interpretation of that picture. Should the picture be unclear, vague or too complex then you may not be able or have time to interpret it and will consequently not respond as I would want. Even if correct interpretation is possible I might not allow you sufficient time to make your response and the deception would fail. So it is most important that I present you with a clear picture which I know you will recognise and then allow time for you to make the desired interpretation of that picture and respond to it. If I do so then I may be able to manipulate your responses to my advantage.

I remember one international player some years ago who usually possessed very subtle deception at the net. His intention was to draw the opponent into the net and then flick the shuttle over his head to the rear-court. This he achieved normally with several flourishes of his racket. On one occasion his opponent could make no sense of these flourishes and not appreciating the pretence, didn't respond. He stood there in the midcourt watching this act until the flick came, which he gratefully smashed down for a winner. The international player could never quite grasp why his deception failed. The outcome of deception must be that the opponent actually makes the *wrong* response in the situation and allows the hitter to outwit him.

When to use deception

Deception has a tactical basis and consequently should be used to create situations to your advantage. The following familiar examples show this:

1. When the shuttle is high in my rearcourt or midcourt, if I look as if to smash, I can cause you to adopt a defensive stance which makes it less easy to move quickly to the rearcourt or forecourt. I could then hit an attack-clear or check-smash and force a weak return.
2. When the shuttle is low in the midcourt and you are threatening to attack I can look as if to return the shuttle to your left or right side, or to the forecourt or rearcourt, and cause you to transfer your weight in the opposite direction to my actual hit.

3. In the forecourt I can look as if to make a net reply, draw you in and create an opening for the flick over your head.

There are two points to consider when using deception in different situations. First, it is most effective if you look as if to play the most attacking move in that situation for that is the main threat which any sensible opponent must cover. Second, always have the racket prepared to make the stroke-move as you approach the shuttle. In this way you can pause during the stroke with the racket in the preparation phase and so create the illusion of 'holding the shot'. The opponent can then be tempted to anticipate your move.

Deception and anticipation

Anticipation takes place when you move prior to the hit in the belief that I intend to make a particular stroke-move. I am successful if I can persuade you to judge wrongly. Most good players try to 'read' the game and anticipate the opponent's probable move. That is why a good deceptive player can be most successful. But because of this it is possible to develop what we might call 'neutral' deception. Rather than looking as if to make one type of move, e.g. the smash, I could prepare to hit the shuttle from the rear-court and not look as if to make any particular move, thus presenting you with a neutral picture from which you can obtain no information. In this way I can create some doubt and uncertainty in your mind and make you wait until the shuttle is hit before you can travel to it.

To achieve this effect I require an identical preparation for similar types of strokes, e.g. forehand overhead, backhand overhead etc. Rudi Hartono is an excellent example of this type of player. In most situations he prepared early and then simply waited until the last moment before hitting the shuttle. Opponents found it difficult to read his probable move and had to wait until the hit before they dared move.

Those players who develop unnecessary stroke habits tend to provide their opponents with sufficient information to enable them to interpret the picture correctly and anticipate the stroke-move. To avoid this all players should, at least, try to simplify their hitting technqiues and make the preparation for similar groups of strokes look identical. Such refinement would go a long way towards helping you acquire the art of deception.

Learning deception

Many players already possess simple efficient strokes and have the basic ingredients for deception. But the essence of deception is that the opponent is deceived. To learn deception you must develop a particular attitude towards the game. You should appreciate the value of it as a tactical aid and develop skilful use of the racket. There should be an inherent enjoyment in cleverly outwitting the opponent, to trick him and entice him into making a futile response. Above all, you must be able to relate what you do to the opponent. He is the focus of your attention and the one who must be thrown off balance, sent the wrong way, held to the spot, fooled and deceived sufficiently to increase your chances of winning the rally. There should be no danger of indulging in too much deception as long as you remember that its purpose is purely tactical.

To learn deception you must practise it, and its practice can only occur in the game. Here you must look as if to do one thing, and then do another; begin a smash and conclude with a drop shot, look as if to flick and change it to a net jab, sway one way and send the shuttle the other. Above all, take a delight in catching the opponent out. The tactical use of deception might just add that bit of extra needed to raise your practical standard of performance in the game.

Percentage play

One further aspect of your development as a player is to play a 'percentage' game. This can be done in several ways.

1.   To perform a 'safe' stroke-move in a situation, reduce the possibility of making an error and yet give no advantage to the opponent. Examples of this are:

1. Hitting to the rearcourt   You can reduce error by aiming the shuttle to specific areas of the court. Too many players hit the shuttle too close to the side lines. What is more important in hitting to the rearcourt is the length rather than the direction.

Rearcourt to rearcourt

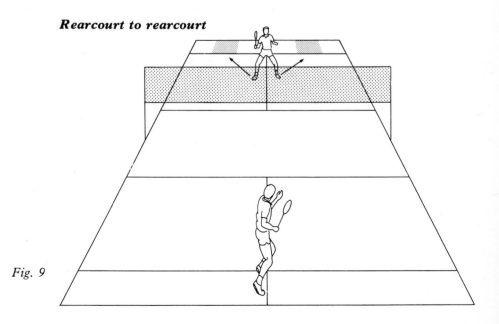

Fig. 9

The clear from the rearcourt is 'safe' if aimed to land in the centre of the opponent's rearcourt. Aim here for both the attack clear and the standard clear. There is still sufficient angle to force the opponent to travel wide out of position to make his reply. As you become more accurate you can aim the shuttle even wider to force the opponent further out of position.

Note: the same area can be aimed for when making a lob reply to the smash.

Forecourt to rearcourt

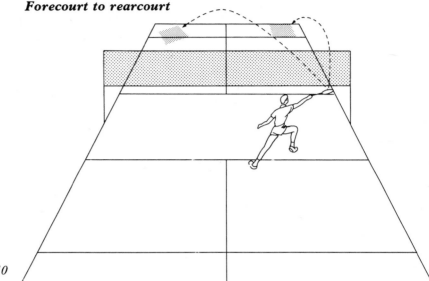

Fig. 10

The lob or whip replies played from below net level in the forecourt are 'safe' if aimed for the areas shown. Both targets allow a greater margin for error when playing the move in the situation. The diagram illustrates the moves from the forehand forecourt. Simply reverse the directions for moves played from the backhand rearcourt.

2. Hitting to the forecourt

Shuttles hit towards the forecourt travel either slowly or quickly through the air. It is bad policy generally to hit 'slow' shuttles across the court for usually the opponent has time to reach the shuttle and lots of space in which to make his reply. The general rule is to play a percentage move and hit straight or to the centre towards the opponent with fast or slow replies, and across the court away from the opponent with fast replies only (see diagrams on the following page).

Rearcourt to forecourt

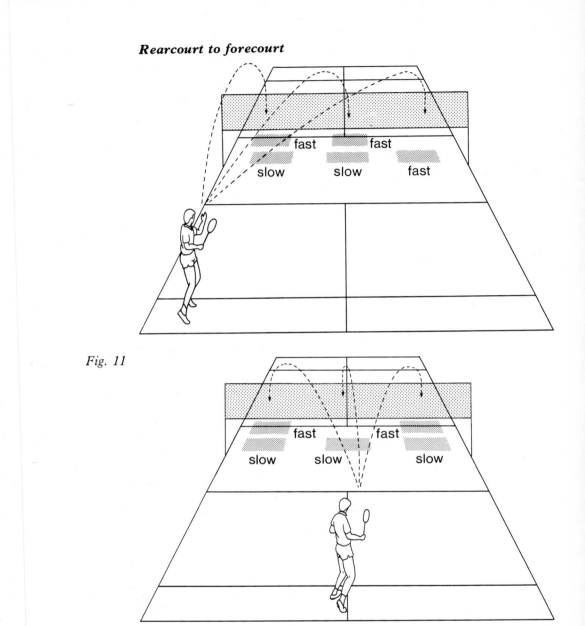

Fig. 11

There should be no difficulty if you remember that the use of the drop shot as a tactical move is to force the opponent to lift the shuttle for you to hit down. The closer the shuttle falls to the net and the later the opponent is in making his reply, the greater is your advantage.

Midcourt to forecourt

The same general rule applies in reply to the smash. Moves towards the opponent may be 'slow' or 'fast' depending on the situation. Moves away from the opponent should be 'fast' if you want to make a percentage move.

2. To create a situation either before or after the opponent's move which reduces his chances of gaining any advantage with his move in the situation. An example of doing so before the opponent makes his move is:

3. Deep defence It is a problem for many players to cope with an opponent who has a powerful smash and is also deceptive when making moves from high in the rearcourt. It is normal practice to adopt a defensive stance in the midcourt and brace yourself for the smash. Quite often this allows the opponent to use the check-smash or the attack clear to catch you out and force a reply to his advantage. The problem is that you are trying to cover all three moves from your position in the midcourt.

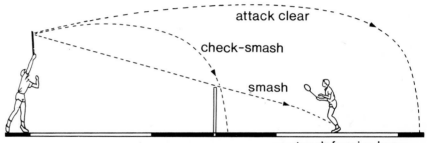

Fig. 12

centre defensive base

It is quite often the case that you might be caught out by the check-smash and the attack clear and though you manage to reach the shuttle it is usually too late to do much with it and your opponent retains his advantage. He keeps you under pressure. One solution is to take up a deep defensive position (see below).

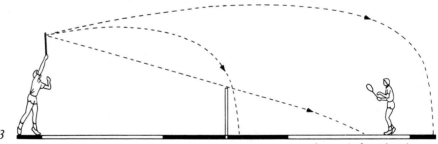

Fig. 13

deep defensive base

To do this you simply move your base further back. There are several advantages in doing this. Firstly, you eliminate his attack clear for, if he now played it, you could just step back and smash it. Secondly, you have more time to see the smash and reply to it. The shuttle decelerates quite rapidly and is easier to reply to the further back you are. There is one obvious disadvantage, for now you have exposed your forecourt to the check-smash and the fast drop shot or angled sliced smash. This situation, however, is not as bad as it may appear for, if you consider for a moment, you will still be able to reach the shuttle in time to make your move. This is because, in deep defence, your stance is not so set in position. You can take a more relaxed (though alert) and upright stance ready to travel forwards quickly to make a reply from the forecourt. Additionally, because you are further back in the court and less braced, you can watch the opponent and judge earlier what move he is likely to make. And you only have a few replies to worry about, for you have eliminated the threat of the power smash or the attack clear. Nor should you concern yourself with the fact that you may take the shuttle late. It is unlikely that you will ever travel so quickly from a defensive position to the forecourt to make a reply from above net height. Unless, of course, your opponent hits a very high floating dropshot as a move, or you reach the degree of athleticism that will enable you to surge forwards to attack the opponent's smash from above the net. Hence it is quite usual to take the shuttle late in this situation. In fact it can be a deliberate policy in percentage play to take the shuttle late. Sometimes doing so will enable you to create situations which are to your advantage or eliminate any advantage the opponent might have gained. Examples of doing this after the opponent has made his move are:

4. Taking the shuttle late in the forecourt

We can continue here from your previous situation and assume that you have indeed arrived late to make your reply. Late perhaps, but because you have chosen to be so. The reason for this is that you want to be in balance and able to play a controlled reply. Often, the desire to take the shuttle early can cause you to lose balance and control of your movements as you hit the shuttle, sometimes resulting in a hasty action and causing either an error, or an ineffective move, often to your disadvantage. To choose to be late is to adopt an attitude of mind, an acceptance of the situation that you will be late anyway so there is no point in rushing to 'attack' the shuttle. In any case, the notion of the 'principle of attack' is that at all times you should try to create a situation in which it is possible to make a scoring blow. There are times, as in this situation, when this is achieved more effectively by taking the shuttle late than by trying to take it early.

When you arrive in balance there are several replies possible, depending on how late you have arrived. If the shuttle is only midway down the net you have a range of replies you can make. Check the chart for these. If you are late and the shuttle is near the ground you might find your replies limited, especially if the opponent is perched ready to attack any net reply. In this situation a 'safe' reply is to lob the shuttle high to the rearcourt. It is important that you hit it high and far enough to allow you *sufficient time* to recover into a deep base position to prepare for your opponent's next move. If you send a shallow lob your opponent will be able to make his move before you are ready and you will be at a disadvantage. If you do not hit the shuttle to the back of the rearcourt he will be able to attack you from nearer the net with more effect. Again you will be at a disadvantage and will have lost all you had hoped to gain by taking the shuttle late.

5. **Taking the shuttle late in the rearcourt** There are occasions when your opponent hits the shuttle past you into the rearcourt. Sometimes you will find it possible to get into the 'smash position', or jump backwards to hit the shuttle, land and still have sufficient time to recover to cover your opponent's replies. At other times it may not be possible to get into the 'smash position' or recover quickly enough from a backward jump smash to cover the replies effectively. On such occasions it is percentage play to take the shuttle late. You would allow the shuttle to get behind you and nearer the ground to enable you to get into a balanced position to play a controlled reply (see plate 14). The stroke-move is made with the weight backwards on the rear foot, a position the player retains throughout the stroke. Most players do allow the shuttle to drop lower and take it late in the backhand rearcourt as they settle down to make their reply. More players could certainly benefit from this type of percentage play in the forehand rearcourt.

3. To take a calculated risk in situations when you anticipate a 'certain' reply.

There are occasions in the game when you create a situation in the hope of anticipating a 'certain' reply. If you intend to play a percentage game you must be reasonably sure that your stroke-move will have the desired effect more often than not. An example of this is the use of the power smash. Played from inside the rearcourt as a move there are a number of replies to the smash. The opponent can block to the forecourt, push the shuttle to the midcourt, and whip and lob it to the rearcourt. If you rush forwards to attack the reply it is more likely that you would be placed at a disadvantage by the lob or whip replies. That is why it is safe policy to hang back after the smash to cover all possible replies from the opponent, even if doing so means that you have to take the replies to the forecourt slightly later.

This is not necessary when the shuttle is high in the midcourt or just short of the rearcourt. A player with a powerful smash can hit the shuttle very hard and literally 'charge' into the forecourt to attack the shuttle as it crosses the net. There are a number of factors which make this possible. Firstly, it is usually advisable to smash at the opponent's backhand or straight to him. As this power smash is hit from relatively near the net the shuttle is still travelling very fast when it reaches the opponent, which is not surprising when it leaves the racket at over 220 miles per hour. The opponent must guard against the smash to his forehand and his backhand and so holds the racket in front of his body ready to hit from either side.

In such a situation most players use a forehand grip and find it easier to make replies from the forehand side than the backhand side. Thus a player might find it possible to flick the shuttle high to the rearcourt or hit it across the court away from the smasher. In which case the 'charge' becomes rather a foolish tactic to adopt.

The power smash is more difficult to reply to from the backhand side. Most players are only capable of making the block reply straight to the net. It is even difficult to angle the reply across the court. Hence the smasher can make his move and 'charge' forwards in anticipation of this 'certain' reply. More often than not he might be correct in his judgement.

Such a tactic is quite possible at the international level of play. I remember some years ago watching Ray Stevens receiving this treatment from Derek Talbot. Ray used almost a panhandle forehand grip in defence and rarely (at that time) changed it to a backhand grip for defence. Consequently, if he was late in preparing to hit the shuttle from the backhand side, he found it difficult to apply much force with his racket. The most he could do was play a straight block reply to the forecourt. Derek Talbot was always an excellent tactician and used to set Ray Stevens up for this reply. He began with a deceptive drop shot to Stevens' forehand forecourt, forcing Stevens to lift the shuttle high by threatening to attack the net. Stevens would lob the shuttle up by using his forehand grip and recover quickly to defend. Talbot, now in position, having played for the lift, would hit a power smash to Stevens' backhand side and charge forwards to attack the reply to the net. More often than not he was able to kill the shuttle and win the rally outright on such occasions. Needless to say, eventually Ray Stevens improved his defence to prevent any opponent exploiting him in this way.

There are many situations in which it becomes possible to play a percentage game. What type of percentage game you play depends on the ability and style of play of both you and your opponent at the time. What is important to realise is that it is something all players can begin to try out from the start and whatever the level of play.

Strategy, tactics and styles of play

Badminton is a game played by people of all shapes and sizes, levels of intelligence and personalities. It is also a game that allows a tremendous variety of ways to be used to defeat the opponent. It is not surprising, therefore, that there are many different styles of play and combinations of stroke-moves in recognisable patterns of play. Though most good players can perform, if necessary, the full range of stroke-moves listed in the charts, they tend to select and combine into patterns those stroke-moves which suit their particular style of play. Thus, though they will make appropriate stroke-moves in accordance with the principle of attack, they put their own 'stamp' on their selection.

What you should try to do is adopt a strategy to contend with the different styles of player and use the most effective tactics (stroke-moves) to win. Most probably you will have your own style which will be seen in the pattern of stroke-moves you select to defeat particular types of opponent. As each individual is unique and has his own individual style it is difficult to lay down any hard and fast rules about how to play. But it is helpful to identify a few different types and perhaps suggest a possible strategy on which to base your stroke-moves. You might be familiar with some of the types described below.

1. The strong player   There are two types of strong player:

a. Power at speed

This player smashes at every opportunity and then surges forward, hitting more smashes and hard flat pushes until he can either hit the winner from the midcourt or forecourt, or force an error.

Strategy. Slow him down and make him less eager to surge forwards and then outmanoeuvre him by playing to his weaknesses.

Tactics. Let him come at you and take the shuttle late to give you time to hit it away from him or back to the rearcourt where he has travelled from. This will wrong-foot him and catch him out. Once caught he will be hesitant about rushing forwards and perhaps may hang back in his rearcourt to anticipate your lob over his head. Then you can drop to his forecourt to gain the lift or hit it cross-court to make him stretch and run. If you can move him around and keep the rally going he may eventually run out of steam and give you the chance to attack him.

b. Power with weight

This is the strong man with the heavy penetrating smash from the rearcourt. He is happier in the rearcourt and midcourt. In the forecourt too much depends on quick movement and touch so he will be quite content to play for a lift with a tumbler or spinner to the centre of the forecourt or lob the shuttle high to your rearcourt and then settle in his midcourt whilst you smash. For this he has developed a good defence and will block the smash to the forecourt to get the lift he wants. Then he will use his powerful smash from the midcourt or rearcourt. He is not too keen about getting involved in long rallies and plays only to get the lift for his smash.

Strategy. Give him nothing to hit and unsettle him.

Tactics. Give him few opportunities to smash effectively by pushing flat or hitting down frequently to his midcourt so that he must lift. If he blocks to the forecourt you require deception, to look as if to play a forecourt reply to draw him in, and then flick the shuttle over his head in a basic move to the rearcourt. You need to move him from the rearcourt to the forecourt and side to side with quick attack clears to the sides and fast sliced drops. Thus he will not be able to settle down into his normal pattern. Deception is most important against this player. If you are quick you can keep him under pressure and unsettled by making early moves and not giving him time to recover.

2. The runner   This is the type of player who enjoys travelling around the court and does so making basic moves to the rearcourt and forecourt with occasional smashes to the midcourt. He likes the open game as he tries to manoeuvre you out of position.

Strategy. Pin him down and restrict his game.

Tactics. The strong player will simply hit through him, for a forceful controlled power attack will defeat him.

   The smash is the most effective move if the opening is made by hitting at him in the centre so as to make it difficult for him to hit to the corners of the

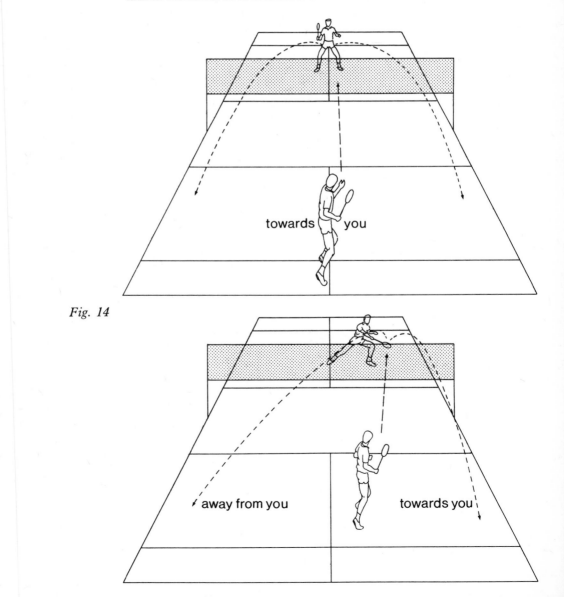

Fig. 14

forecourt and rearcourt, therefore giving him no angle, and narrowing the direction of his return. This move ensures that he makes his reply towards you instead of away from you (see fig. 14).

Thus he cannot manoeuvre you around so easily. It is also effective to clear to his centre rearcourt for the same reason. A forecourt situation with spinners and tumblers will tend to restrict his game and force the lift or a weak reply for you to smash at him. In general his game is very predictable and the moves very simple. The rule is not to get caught up in long rallies but maintain the principle of attack and create situations to make scoring hits.

3. The fast attacking player This is the type who keeps up a very high rate of play, travelling to meet the shuttle early and giving his opponent little time to recover from his moves. He hits fast drops and steep angled sliced smashes to the forecourt/midcourt area, power smashes to the midcourt both straight and cross-court, and fast attack clears to the corners of the rearcourt. He is an extremely difficult player to defeat.

Strategy. Upset his rhythm, slow him down and exploit any weaknesses.

Tactics. He usually recovers very quickly and travels into position to cover the possible replies, so keeping you very contained and under pressure.
a.   Slow the game down by hitting high defensive clears to the centre of his rearcourt from your rearcourt and forecourt if you are under pressure. This way you can keep control and give him time to think, which he doesn't want. He wants to get on with the game at his tempo. For this you need a good defence and the ability to accelerate quickly from the defensive stance in the midcourt to the rearcourt or forecourt.
b.   Make the unexpected move and switch the shuttle around with angled directions and straight replies to the rearcourt, midcourt and forecourt.
c.   Vary the pace by pushing flat to the midcourt and by taking the speed off the shuttle and hitting it softly to the forecourt.
d.   Use deception to delay his anticipation, create doubt and upset his flow.

4. The touch player He likes to play the game around the forecourt and midcourt, where he can angle his block to the smash and get into the forecourt to make difficult tumblers and spinners, or flick off the top of the net past you to the rearcourt and use his deception with good effect. He doesn't do much from the rearcourt except try to set up the situation in the forecourt.

Strategy. Keep the pressure on him and move him to the rearcourt.

Tactics. Hit fast flat midcourt moves down the sides and at him to crowd him and keep him under pressure. In the forecourt either hit down quickly or keep alert and threaten his replies, so forcing a lift rather than one of his touch shots. If you cannot hit down, lift to the rearcourt and move him away from the forecourt where he is more dangerous.

These examples do not do justice to the full range of possibilities in styles of play or the way in which the same player may mix several styles of play to overcome the opponent. But they do give some idea of how the stroke-moves can be adapted to carry out various strategies. In each of the examples there is one more alternative and that is to match the opponent at his game. But that depends very much on your physical build and attitude to the game. A small light player would not equal a strong player, nor could the strong heavy player equal the runner. So it does raise the question of whether there is a perfect type for badminton: a player who is fast, strong, powerful, agile, athletic, with endurance and good control and touch, who can combine stroke-moves and play whatever type of game suits his purpose. A tall player, like Morten Frost, the Danish 1982 All England Champion (see plate 36), with these attributes would have more advantage than a small player. However, whatever your build, any success is most unlikely unless you can learn to defeat your opponent; and to do that you must be able to use your stroke-moves effectively against each opponent.

Thus you must possess the technical and tactical skill to do so. This you can develop with continual practice in situations which you can work out from the charts. The test of whether you are up to standard comes from playing opponents, for here you learn what you can do to the opponent and what he can do to you, i.e. your relative strengths and weaknesses.

Now to complete your development as a player you need to know how and what to practise and how to assess your progress in the game. The next two chapters deal with these aspects of the game.

Plate 36. Morten Frost

Chapter 8 Practice Makes Perfect

The purpose of practice is to improve your performance in a particular aspect of the game. Usually it is associated with the strokes, footwork and the use of strokes as tactical moves. The game, however, also requires that you are fit to do the work and possess the right sort of positive attitude to win. Practices can be devised to improve your fitness and attitude at the same time as you develop your technical and tactical skills.

Technical and tactical practices are inter-related forms of practice. *In a technical practice the emphasis is on you and how you perform. In a tactical practice it is on your opponent and what you do to him.* You would practise your strokes and footwork separately or together simply as a means to learn or improve them. You might, for example, extract a specific stroke or footwork pattern from the game, e.g. the forehand smash, backhand clear, the lunge and recovery, or the landing and push off after the backward jump smash. Your practice of any of these aspects would help you to reach a satisfactory technical standard. Then you could switch your attention to its use in the performance of a stroke-move in a situation in the game. You could now devise a tactical practice. Here the whole pattern of movement becomes important, i.e. your starting position, travel to the new situation, the stroke-move and the recovery to cover any possible replies. The thing that matters most is what your stroke-move does to the opponent. The difference is that, whereas before you practised 'the clear' to improve your technical execution of the stroke (as a stroke), now you hit the clear as a stroke-move to the rearcourt, and judge it by the effect it has on your practice partner or opponent. Does it go over his head quickly? Does it make him travel quickly all the way to the rearcourt? Does it place him the furthest distance from the net and so create space? Does it make it difficult for him to get behind the shuttle to smash and recover quickly? Does it force him to reply with a clear rather than a smash? Do you recover after your clear stroke-move to cover his possible replies?

It is quite easy to see how a tactical practice may include work in several different situations. This is because the stroke-move cannot be practised in isolation, as can the stroke. In a tactical practice you have to devise a practice in which you begin in one situation, travel to the rearcourt to make your clear-move and then recover by travelling to a new position to cover the possible replies to your clear.

Practice routines are quite usual in the learning of badminton these days. Unfortunately the quality of performance in practice so often falls below standard, not because players lack technical ability but because they do not relate the strokes to their function as moves against their partners. Practice only becomes meaningful when it is related to the game. This is because the 'principle of attack' provides the ultimate justification for everything you do in the game, even in practice. When you do a practice be certain that you know the tactical point of it and how you must perform it to improve your tactical play.

Here is a typical sort of practice routine.

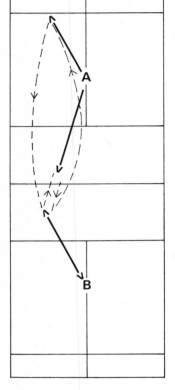

Fig. 15

The sequence is:
B serves to RC
A drops from RC
B plays net reply
A plays net reply
B lifts to RC
A travels to RC and repeats sequence

This is usually badly performed, bearing little resemblance to actual play. The main fault is that players often run backwards and forwards from rearcourt to forecourt and from midcourt to forecourt, quite differently from the way they would move in the game. They do the work and perform the strokes, not as moves in the game but simply to keep the shuttle in play. Often it is immediately obvious to any spectator that the players are only practising, whereas at first sight it should appear as if the players were engaged in a serious game. That they are not should only become apparent after a while, when the spectator realises that the players repeat the same movements and obviously are performing a set practice.

The correct way to do this practice is as follows.
1. Players stand in serving and receiving positions.
2. B serves high to A's RC.
3. A travels back to RC and adopts the 'smash position' to threaten B whilst B recovers to the MC and adopts a defensive stance.
4. A hits a check-smash to FC and walks forward towards the MC to watch B preparing to make his move.
5. B plays a net reply to the FC and recovers into an attacking stance to threaten A and watch his move.
6. A runs forwards as he sees B play the net reply and prepares to hit down from above the net. He cannot and so plays a net reply into B's FC and recovers to an attacking stance to threaten B.
7. B lifts shuttle to A's RC and recovers to the MC to adopt a defensive stance as A travels back to RC into the smash position.
8. Repeat continuously.

In such practice there are pauses as the players make stroke-moves and recover to threaten the opponent. Such a practice is realistic for it is similar in movement and attitude to the tactical play in the game.

All practice should have a tactical basis. If players and their coaches remembered this then there would be a vast improvement in the quality of practice and subsequently in the level of performance in the game.

What is practice?

The most familiar statement about practice is that 'Practice makes perfect.' As we know from experience, this is quite true. But the statement is not quite complete. It misses out a few important words. It should read: 'Practice makes perfect what you practise.' For you can practise incorrectly just as easily, if not more so, as you can correctly.

Practice involves the repetition of some part of the game. We repeat things to get them right. When we have done so, we no longer have to think about how we perform. It becomes a habit. Unfortunately, it is all too easy to develop bad habits. This can even occur when you are learning to get something right. For if it is not right initially you cannot help but repeat partially the incorrect way to do something until you eventually attain the correct way. The constant repetition can 'groove in' incorrect ways of doing things just as easily as correct ways. If, for example, you practised the forehand smash using a 'panhandle' grip and a bent arm pushing action, instead of throwing the racket head at the shuttle, then it would be the bent arm push you would make perfect rather than what you originally intended.

Try to make all practices quality practices. Develop correct habits from the start, although, as has been suggested, this can be a slow process. For in learning the correct way, you will be trying to alter some of the incorrect things you do, and this takes time. This is why a 'good' coach is useful, for he can pinpoint errors and guide you towards the most effective way from the start. I should point out here that there is no *one* best way of doing something. The best way is what works for you and enables you to play the game effectively. If you can make all the stroke-moves necessary to defeat any opponent by gripping the racket with your teeth or your toes then that is right for you – though obviously, since we are human, some methods are more effective than others. What is important for any improvement is *how* you practise. Most players, with or without coaches, perform stroke practices and tactical situation practices, but they do not really practise. *They do practices without practising.* It is all too easy to perform a practice routine which lacks quality, has the effect of making perfect bad habits, and results in a lowering rather than an improvement in your standard of performance in the game.

Let's take an example. A very basic practice is the forehand clear routine. The purpose of the clear is to send the shuttle high to the opposite rearcourt to place the opponent out of position as far from the forecourt as possible. This creates space and makes it difficult for the opponent to attack. You should know this much about the clear as a move before you commence practice. During the stroke practice you learn the 'clear' and so focus attention on yourself and how you 'clear'. There are a number of ways that you can check that you are doing it correctly as a stroke-move.

1. Do you get into the smash position behind the shuttle ready to smash or dropshot as easily as make the clear?
2. Does the action feel right, smooth, easy and fluent or does it feel awkward and strained?
3. Does the shuttle reach the forecourt by travelling over the opponent and out of his reach?
4. Do you remain in balance as you hit the shuttle and are you able to travel forwards to recover immediately after the stroke-move?

If you could do these things every time you hit the clear in practice then you would always perform a quality practice. For though the emphasis is on how you hit the shuttle, the practice will only become a quality practice if it is purposeful and meaningful, with respect to how you would want to perform the clear as a move in the game. The use of the clear, or any other stroke, as a move in the game, determines how you perform it in practice. Thus even a stroke practice has a tactical basis. If all players remembered this in practice, then we would not see so many clears fail to reach the rearcourt, or players step backwards off-balance after the clear, simply due to lack of care and effort in getting into a position to smash, drop or clear.

Make sure that you practise properly. Check with the charts to find out the tactical basis of the strokes you want to practise. Give it some thought and work out how you would want to perform it in the game. If you are not sure, experiment on the court, miming without a shuttle. Ask a good coach for advice or watch a top-class player in action. Don't watch the game. Just focus all your attention on the player and you will learn much about how to perform in the game. Above all, do not be satisfied with less than your best. *Practise with quality.*

How much should you practise?

The amount and distribution of practice can vary. Much depends on the level you are at and want to reach. It can also vary with respect to the different parts of the game and whether you are learning something new, or keeping some aspect of your game up to standard. Players differ in how much they practise and, apart from accepting that you should practise, there is no fixed rule about how much and when.

You may find that you improve from doing a small amount regularly with small intervals between each practice, e.g. daily or every two days. Or, a large amount on each occasion with longer breaks between each practice. If you have time you might overload and do a lot regularly. You must find your own balance between the amount of practice and the distribution of it. It must be borne in mind that too much practice may risk damage to the joints in the body, particularly of the shoulder and elbow which receive excessive use during stroke practices. I believe that in time there will be scientific evidence to confirm that the repetition of strokes in practice is the major cause of joint injuries. The wear and tear on the joints is increased if the technique is poor for then there is also excessive strain. One way to avoid the risk of joint injury is to emphasise the quality of work in practice to ensure good stroke production. It would help if players concentrated and tried to perform actions correctly, both technically and tactically, during the practice. For example, if you are practising the forehand clear, make a serious effort to hit the shuttle to the opponent's rearcourt accurately and with control on each consecutive hit. If you could do this ten times out of ten on the first occasion then there would be no need to perform a routine practice of 100 clears. A good standard of performance on all occasions could reduce the amount of practice by half and thus the amount of potential damage to the joints.

What can affect practice?

It is difficult to practise well if you lose interest in the practice. New practices can be interesting, making it easier to concentrate and maintain quality in your work. Old familiar routines can easily become boring and so make it more difficult to be conscientious.

To practise well takes discipline, for you must concentrate on the task and maintain the quality. Sometimes, if things aren't going right it may be best to leave that practice and do something else. At other times perseverance may be called for.

In the early period of learning new skills, you may do more practice than later when you practise solely to maintain your standard. You may get tired; it is then all too easy to become sloppy in your work and develop bad habits. If you are unable to maintain your standards at this stage then it is better to stop, rest, or change the practice. Experience, regular work and common sense will provide you with the knowledge of how much and when to practise. Use your common sense and be honest with yourself about your efforts. The test of your practice is whether you improve your game. If you don't, then examine the practice or the way you perform it, and think again. In general, I am sure that you will know what you want to improve. The difficult part is to devise practices which are meaningful and really do improve your skill in playing the game. So let's take a look at how to devise practices in the various aspects of the game.

How to devise a practice

1. **Selection**   First you must decide what aspect of your game you want to improve: for this refer to the charts. Study the situations and the stroke-moves possible. Take each situation in turn and assess what you can or cannot do in each one. Then make a list of things you need to learn or improve. It is important to select practices that you are able to perform and which are interesting and meaningful. This way you will avoid frustration, if they are too difficult, and boredom, if too easy.

Each tactical situation can be broken down into a number of parts. For example, assume that the situation is in the rearcourt. You have travelled there from the midcourt to perform a backhand clear and then recover, travelling back to the midcourt to defend. To do this you complete a pattern of movement, containing a number of parts which you can practise together or separately. These are:

- The push-off and acceleration from the midcourt and the travel phase to the rearcourt
- The arrival to position yourself and prepare to make the stroke-move
- The stroke-move
- The recovery towards the midcourt

You may find that your technique is poor and you cannot hit the backhand clear effectively as a stroke-move. So you extract it from the game situation and work solely on the action of hitting the clear. To do this you could seek help from a coach. However, you may wish to work on your own by miming the action in front of the mirror; carry a racket around the house and practise hitting imaginary shuttles; or go on court with a partner and hit numerous backhand clears until you begin to get it right. Then you would return to the tactical situation and practise it as a stroke-move in the game. This process can apply to any part of the tactical situation. Once the technical practice has helped to improve your technique then quickly switch back to the tactical practice. *Technical practices help you to control and master yourself whereas tactical practices help you to control and master your opponents and are the most important with respect to the game.*

Tactical practices

A stroke-move can be learnt in isolation or in combination with other stroke-moves in a situation. Examples of these are:
1.   Select the power smash and recovery, or combine it with the sliced smash. The practice would require a 'feeder' who feeds single shuttles continuously for you to alternate the power smash and the sliced smash in sequence. An isolated stroke-move or a combined stroke-move can be performed in rearcourt, midcourt and forecourt situations.

2. Select two situations and perform the same stroke or different strokes in each situation. For example, the power smash could be performed from the right side and the left side of the rearcourt within the same practice; or the smash from one side and the attack clear from the other side. This would involve the addition of travelling between situations and so include footwork and balance.

3. Combine different situations and different stroke-moves. For example, you could hit a smash from the rearcourt and then travel forward to play a spinner from the forecourt. All these practices require another player who might act as a 'feeder' and who also practises his stroke-move as replies to your moves. If you look at the total picture, with you making pre-determined moves from one situation and the feeder making replies from another situation, then it would appear that the following situations can be selected for practice.

Single situation practices

Examples are:

Rearcourt to rearcourt
Rearcourt to midcourt
Rearcourt to forecourt
(And of course, the same would apply for the midcourt and forecourt.)

These practices are quite easy to perform. For example, in a rearcourt to rearcourt practice the feeder would hit the shuttle high to your forehand or backhand rearcourt. But you would not simply clear the shuttle back to him: you would have to travel from your midcourt, get into the smash position, hit the clear and then recover to the midcourt to take up a defensive stance. If you hit an attack clear then you might recover quickly. If you hit a high defensive clear you would walk back to the midcourt. However, in addition the feeder would have to work hard. He too must return to his midcourt after each clear. This is because the test of your clear as a stroke-move is the effect it has on the feeder. You have to send him back to his rearcourt, and this you can do quickly (to make him rush), or slowly. Thus, you would watch his feet, as you return to your midcourt, to see if he does place them in the rearcourt to make his reply. If he does, then you know that your clear was effective, in sending him as far out of position as possible. This practice could take the form of single repetitions with a pause between each, or continuous rallying.

Combination situation practices

An example would be:
Rearcourt and forecourt to rearcourt

The feeder would hit the shuttle high to your rearcourt. You would travel quickly from your midcourt to the rearcourt, make the clear to the opposite rearcourt, recover to the midcourt to take up a defensive stance. The feeder would hit a check-smash to your forecourt. You would travel quickly forwards, to clear from your forecourt over the feeder's head to his rearcourt and then recover to take up a defensive stance in your midcourt. End of practice.

This could be repeated until you felt satisfied with your performance. Once again it could be practised in the form of a continuous rally. But if so, it is most important that you do not allow the standard of performance to fall during the practice.

Complex situation practices

Here you would practise moves in a situation and end the rally with a scoring hit. The practice will be designed to allow you to end the rally with a smash from the rearcourt/midcourt area or the kill from the forecourt.

An example is:
Forecourt to forecourt to midcourt

Start in the midcourt. Take up a forward attacking stance. The feeder hits the shuttle from his midcourt into your forecourt. Travel forwards and play a tumbler or spinner and then recover into the attacking stance on the edge of your forecourt. The feeder lifts the shuttle over your head towards the rearcourt.

Travel back quickly and smash the shuttle to his midcourt and recover into an attacking stance in your midcourt.

End of rally. Begin again.

A complex practice includes making stroke-moves and travelling between different situations for you and the 'feeder'. You both have to work hard to perform them correctly and gain the benefit from the practice. After a while it becomes quite easy to select situations which give you experience of making a scoring hit.

There are many advantages of working in this way. From the start the strokes are meaningful as moves in the game. There is the build-up to a conclusion, with the strokes used to create the situation in which you can make the final scoring hit. You will develop confidence in knowing that you can create situations and can go for the winner when the opportunity arises. You will also gain more insight into the connection between situations and the relevance of certain strokes as moves in those situations. This sort of practice is also more enjoyable and interesting, for knowing that there is an end to the practice is an incentive to being totally committed in going for the winner. You know that it is the successful attempt that ends the practice. If you continually practise creating situations where the end is the attempt to make a winning move you will gradually develop a positive approach to the game. You will get used to creating situations which contribute to making a scoring hit. It will become a habit to be adventurous and to take calculated risks when the opportunity arises. A well-designed situation practice will help you to do this.

2. Construction

To construct a practice is generally simple in theory but quite difficult on the court. The difficulties arise in trying to make the practice realistic. To be realistic it must be similar to the actual game situation. Imagine a situation in which you have smashed from the rearcourt and your opponent blocks the smash to the forecourt. Thus the shuttle travels from a low position to cross the net on an upward pathway. You travel into the forecourt and hit the shuttle down for a winner.

Now assume that you want to design a practice with a lunge into the forecourt and a downward hit from the net. How do you begin? You decide that the 'feeder' will feed by hand. There are two points to clarify:
1. Where does the feeder stand in relation to the net?
2. How does he throw the shuttle?

The first question involves shuttle speed and the distance it must travel. This must be decided in order to get the timing right in the practice. The second question is to do with the trajectory of the shuttle flight. Does the feeder use an overarm throw (like a darts player) or does he throw from underarm? In a game you would see the shuttle coming upwards from a low position, so it would be more realistic to feed from that position. Whatever way you decide to feed the shuttle, by hand or racket, give some thought to the trajectory of the shuttle. Always consider the move that created the situation, and the sort of position and actions that you would adopt preceding and following the stroke-move in that situation. Here are some guidelines:
1. Decide on the situation and the stroke-move that you want to practise.
2. Explain the purpose of the practice to the 'feeder'.
3. Work out the starting positions of yourself and the 'feeder'.
4. Write out clear instructions about the order of moves in the practice.
   Note: it helps to draw a sketch of the court, which illustrates the practice, with clear instructions at the side.

I often find that in designing a new practice, I work out the situation and write out the practice on paper. Once on the court it may take some time altering and modifying the design before it will work properly. This is quite usual and is to be expected at times. Below are shown two practices which are taken from typical situations in a game.

First practice

It involves a smash from the rearcourt and the kill in the forecourt. The emphasis is on connecting a rearcourt and forecourt move.

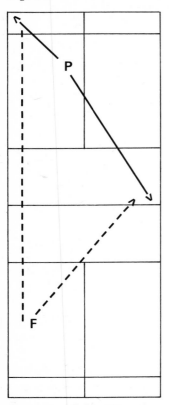

P = player   F = feeder

P faces F and the players stand in the positions as shown.

1. F serves high to the forehand side of P's rearcourt.
2. P travels across and smashes straight. P recovers by travelling towards the midcourt whilst facing F.
3. F replies with a x-court return to the forecourt.
4. P travels quickly forwards and attempts a backhand kill from the net and recovers quickly to an attacking stance in the FC. End of rally.
5. Players get back into position and start again.
6. Complete 10 successful attempts.

It may take you more than 10 attempts to get it right 10 times; so keep at the practice until you *have* got it right 10 times.

Second practice

This practice is designed for a player who is slow to recover from the smash and, therefore, late in getting to the cross-court whip reply to the smash.

Players stand in the positions as shown.

1. F serves high to backhand RC of P.
2. P travels to RC and smashes straight.
3. F whips the shuttle high x-court to the forehand MC of P.
4. P sprints across and attempts a scoring hit, i.e. a smash or a drive. P recovers to an attacking stance in the MC. End of rally.
5. Players get back into position and begin again.
6. Complete 10 successful attempts.

Variations on a practice

There are numerous variations possible in these practices. Variations alter the situations and require different stroke-moves. For example, in the first practice, the feeder could make a straight return to the smash; or you could travel to the forecourt and hit straight or cross-court. Alternatively, the feeder could serve high to the backhand rearcourt. A programme could consist of a number of different practices or variations on a practice.

Evaluation of a practice

Does the practice achieve its purpose and improve your ability in a specific situation? How can you test the success of a practice? There are two basic methods.

1. Count the number of successful attempts out of a set number, e.g. ten.
2. Test it in the game.

Both of these methods are crude because it is not possible to establish ideal conditions for the test. There will always be slight variations in each attempt, i.e. shuttle speed, trajectory, timing of the stroke, etc. In the game these

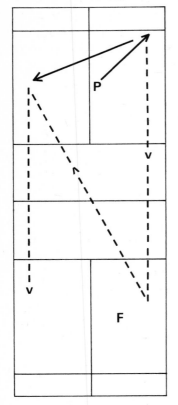

Fig. 17

factors will vary even more. Nevertheless, we can measure the success or failure of a practice sufficiently to say whether it worked or not. Let us apply the methods of testing to the first practice, which was designed to improve your ability to play rearcourt and forecourt moves.

Method 1

The test is to measure the number of successful attempts in a set number of repetitions of the practice. You could do this on a number of occasions over a period of time. If there is an improvement in your degree of success in the tests then we can assume that you have improved your ability to make these particular stroke-moves.

Method 2

This is rather more difficult but still possible to use to measure your progress to some extent. Here you can condition the game to ensure that the situation arises in the game. You simply add a few new rules to the game. For example, you could stipulate that your opponent must always clear to your forehand rearcourt when he does clear, and when you smash straight he must always block cross-court. In this way, you guarantee that the situation will occur and then count the number of successful attempts and failures during the game. *Note:* there is one major weakness in this practice. Knowing that your opponent must block to the forecourt, you can rush forwards and anticipate. To prevent this, you also allow him to return your smash with a clear to the rearcourt occasionally. Now you would be forced to wait before travelling to the forecourt. As a result of the practice of this move you should be able to perform it successfully if it occurs in a contest.

Performing under pressure in practice

In a game you are often under pressure and have to do a large amount of work in a short period of time. You may have to travel quickly from one situation to another and recover very quickly from the stroke-moves you play. Consequently there should be emphasis on developing speed. The ability to perform well under pressure requires good technique and a high level of fitness.

One simple but effective way to add pressure is to speed up the rate of working. There are several methods that can be used. The most obvious way is to use faster shuttles. If you use the highest speeds, then normal reaction time, stroke production and general movement around the court all have to speed up. This also has the beneficial effect of developing concentration, increasing explosive acceleration from one situation to another and finally, in the game situation, it makes the normal pace shuttle appear to travel much more slowly.

Another way is to hit hard smashes from the midcourt and so reduce the recovery time in defence; or hit a hard flat smash from the rearcourt and reduce recovery time to reach the reply to the smash; or hit flatter clears to the rearcourt. The rest time between each repetition of the practice can be reduced to increase pressure in fitness training on the court. For more information on this aspect of the game, refer to *Get Fit for Badminton* (see p. 83), which contains detailed explanations and advice on how to work under pressure. The most important point to remember is that all pressure training is based on the principle of overload. Once you grasp this it is quite easy to work out ways to overload your practice of the various aspects of the game.

Practice and competition

So far the practices have been constructed from situations which actually occur in the game. Various parts have been isolated and extracted from the game to enable you to practise them. Now arrives the time when you have to return to the game and apply what you have learned in practice. Unfortunately, unless you are alert, this could make your game worse rather than better. If you have been doing technical practices you may meet a problem during the game. For in technical practice, the focus is on yourself rather than on the opponent. This explains why one sees so many young players who, as a result of numerous stroke routines, seem to be more concerned with playing strokes than opponents. They do not use the strokes as moves in the game. There should be no such problem if you have been doing tactical practices for these always relate to what you do to an opponent. When you play the game you have got used to focusing on the opponent in practice.

Just to remind you of this, examine the stages below which show the progression from practice to competition.

Stage 1
Use the charts to examine your game for weaknesses and parts that should be learnt. Isolate them and extract them from the game.

Stage 2
Devise and perform practices
a. technical – strokes and footwork
b. tactical – stroke-moves and recovery with travelling between situations

Stage 3
Return to the game. Play games and apply what you have practised in the game.

This final stage is also difficult for other reasons. It takes confidence to try out something new or what was a previous weakness, in a contest. It doesn't follow that just because you have worked hard on something in practice you can immediately use it in the game. It would be marvellous if this was so but, in general, for the majority of us, it doesn't happen quite like that. So, unless you are an exception to the rule, don't be surprised if your game does not immediately reach new levels of excellence. You may easily have doubts about whether what you have practised will stand the test, particularly if the game is a tough one. Then it would not be surprising if you played safe and reverted to familiar well-established habits.

Your confidence, in applying practice to play, depends on the extent to which it has become a part of your 'natural' game and an intuitive, automatic response in a situation. This, in turn, depends on the amount of meaningful work you have done in practice. The final factor which might affect your confidence is the opponent. You will certainly know if something is not a part of your 'natural' game if you meet a tough opponent. He will make you very conscious of any weakness, for he provides you with the hardest test of your practice.

So let's assume that you have worked very hard on tactical situation practices and that these have been meaningful and realistic. Now you must make the big jump between practice and play. Well, luckily, you don't have to jump all the way. There are a few ways of bridging the gap. You could devise a *conditioned game*. This is similar to a normal game except that extra rules are added to make certain that you use the practised part in the game. For example: imagine that you have been practising at developing your speed in travelling to the rearcourt to get into the smash position. You now play a game but add an extra rule, i.e. you are only allowed to smash from high in the rearcourt. If you break the rule by doing a clear or a drop then you lose the rally.

Or, assume that you have been practising the replies to the forecourt from the forecourt. This requires much skill and, often, courage to take the opponent on at the net in the game. So we make you do it. Add an extra rule to the game: 'you are now allowed to lift to the midcourt or rearcourt when the shuttle is below net level in your forecourt'. It is quite obvious that if your opponent knows the rule he will try to drop to the forecourt and then travel in and wait poised to kill any poor replies above net level. It will certainly force you to take care and play with control and accuracy in the game.

To some extent conditioned games make your practice an automatic part of your game. But you know it is not the real game, and for that you need to play opponents in competition, when you play according to the normal rules of the game.

There are two types of competitive play: friendly games and formal competition (organised games, tournaments etc.). A friendly game is the best place to try to incorporate your practice, as nothing hangs upon the result of a friendly game. This is your best chance to try out ideas in competitive play. Here you would try to win, but not at the expense of developing your game. Thus you would use your practice in play as much as possible; even though it is still rather new and uncertain to you, and might cause you to make an error and lose the rally. But, if you are sensible and forward looking, this wouldn't matter. You would realise that the more you tried out a stroke-move in friendly competition, the easier it would be to do so in serious competition.

In formal competition, the emphasis must be on winning. Trying to win is a serious business. It is a test of your badminton skill against another player's skill. Nevertheless, there is still the occasional opportunity to practise in play. But to do so can be risky. You must be careful and sensible about it. One international player I worked with used the earlier rounds of the tournament to practise parts of his game. There were several ways he did this. If he was playing a weaker opponent and stood a fair chance of winning, he took every opportunity to practise a new stroke-move in the situation, even to the extent of putting himself into 'impossible' situations. He felt safe in doing this because he knew that his weaker opponent could not create much pressure on him. If he won the first game he would continue this way throughout the match. In fact, sometimes he went so far as to give his opponent the chance to place him under pressure. For example, he might deliberately hit a weak clear to the midcourt to allow the opponent to smash for a winner, so that he could practise his speed and control in defence. Another time he might drop to the forecourt and then stay right back to invite a return to the forecourt; then travel forwards to take the shuttle late, from near the ground, and make a return to the forecourt with his opponent waiting ready to attack the weak reply. You try it sometime, it can be quite a challenge.

If, however, he began to lose too many points and the opponent seemed to become a threat to his success then he would quickly revert to his former familiar 'winning' game against that opponent. He would continue in this way until he met a respected strong opponent. Then the emphasis was solely on winning in the most thorough and efficient way, i.e. playing the type of game with which he was most familiar.

Nevertheless, with continuous play in this way, the new stroke-move would become an accepted part of his total game. He found that he was able to use it intuitively as an automatic response in a situation. Such an approach to competition applies not only to international players: it applies equally well to anyone who wants to become a better player. So give it some thought and find ways of relating your practice in play.

A positive approach to practice

I have continually emphasised that you should make moves in a situation according to the principle of attack. Such an approach to the game is very positive. You can only play in this way if you know what you are trying to do on the court, and if you are prepared to be imaginative and adventurous. Thus in practice you should be willing to experiment, along with a total commitment to 'having a go' when the chance arises. You will find that in formal competition, there may be more safe 'percentage' play and less taking of chances. Particularly if you reckon that an extra stroke-move will serve to create a better situation in which to attack. For example, you might get a faint chance to kill a shuttle above net level in the forecourt. But you decide that this is just too risky, for the chance of making an error or not recovering to cover a reply is too great. So, you play a tumbler very close to the net, recover to an attacking stance on the edge of the forecourt and threaten the reply to the forecourt. Thus you force a possible mis-hit or a steep weak lift to the midcourt. From there you have a safe chance of hitting a winner.

In practice nothing is lost by 'having a go'. There is, however, a vast difference between 'having a go' in the sense of being adventurous, rather than reckless. Recklessness is a sign of either ignorance or stupidity. One can make mistakes in ignorance and learn from the experience. Stupidity is the mark of the fool who continually fails to learn from his experience. When you are adventurous you maintain some degree of control. Even so, if the practice is difficult, you will most probably make quite a few errors at the start. If you are practising the jump lunge and kill off the net then expect to make a few errors. As you get used to the action and learn control, you will begin to make more winners than errors. This is why practising is so important. You can repeat your stroke-moves and correct your errors until you get things right. Only by attempting something can you learn to do it. You learn to be adventurous by being adventurous. You learn to attack by attacking.

It is only by continual persistent practice in situations in which the attack is always attempted that even the faintest chance will become a strong possibility of making a winning hit. If you work hard in this way, then your confidence should increase as it becomes a habit to attack successfully when the opportunity arises.

I remember one particular tournament, when Rudi Hartono was four match points down to Sture Johnsson in the semi-final. Hartono saved the first match point, reduced them to three and then lost his serve for Johnsson to serve with three match points. The tension was almost unbearable, for everyone in the stadium had focused on this match. Hartono cleared, Johnsson smashed, Hartono blocked to the net. Johnsson came in and played a tight spinning reply close to the net. Hartono leaped forwards to attack the faint possibility (see plate overleaf). He could drop to the forecourt or lift to the rearcourt, both safe percentage moves. Instead he went for the kill and got it. The crowd were amazed. Johnsson was overawed. Hartono, match points down and going for his chances without compromise. What character! Yes, but such adventurous play could only result from the knowledge that he could kill the shuttle as was his usual custom. The years spent in practising attacking badminton on the practice court and match court paid off at the crucial moment. He won that match.

Plate 37.
Rudi Hartono

Practice and the coach

If you have a coach, then be aware of some of the disadvantages that affect developing a positive attacking attitude. The majority of coaches are conventional and therefore conform to accepted safe ways of doing things. Coaching can be negative in its approach. The coach is trying to bring you up to some standard which, at the present time, you are below. Consequently, many of his comments may be on the negative side and about the things you are doing wrong rather than those you do right. Without realising it, it is easy for the coach to develop a negative attitude in your approach to the game. This will become apparent as we take a look at what the coach should do to develop a positive attitude to the game. He must create the right atmosphere for you to be adventurous. In the early stages the attempt, not the result, is most important. You can expect to experience more failure than success when learning a difficult task. For this reason it is more beneficial for you if the coach encourages you to be adventurous and praises your efforts rather than comment on your failures. In this way, with constant exposure to the situation and careful refinement of your technique you should begin to gain success. Consequently your confidence should increase in the knowledge that you can contend with such a situation. During this period, in both practice and competition, the coach should maintain his constant encouragement, with his comments about your attempts to do the right thing rather than your results.

There are many coaches who do not praise or encourage their players to have a go in practice. These coaches usually criticise their players for failing in the attempt. As a result, such players lack the confidence or the courage to take a chance when it arises. It's not difficult to understand why. Few players are prepared to expose themselves to criticism, so few will risk getting into a situation in which there is little guarantee of success and a high chance of failure; failure only brings criticism. Criticism doesn't have to be spoken; any negative behaviour, gesture, expression and even silence can be taken as criticism. If this occurs, players know and feel it, and become less prepared to be adventurous. They fall into a 'play safe' approach in a situation unless, of course, there is absolutely no way of failing to make a scoring hit. Eventually the idea of being adventurous, going for the winner when the opportunity arises, is neglected, and so is the positive approach to the game. The strokes are not used effectively as moves designed to create situations which eventually increase one's chances of making a scoring hit. The player ends up a safe player whose future development is limited. The game at the present time is filled with coached players who possess skilful strokes and footwork. They are a credit to the work of the coach on the technical aspects of the game. Unfortunately, for the majority, that is all that can be said for them. The rest of their game reflects a negative approach, 'play safe', dull, mediocre, conformist, monotonous, unexciting play which, tactically, is boring to watch. If you are a coach, look critically at the implications of your teaching methods and your attitude to the game. Reflect on what is required to play attacking badminton and whether your work actually achieves that effect – that is, if you agree that badminton is an attacking game.

If you are a player there are several alternatives open to you. You can ignore, educate or leave your coach. It is important that you do something. For in the competitive arena, all things being equal, it is the player who is positive and takes his chances who will be the winner. And even if you do not win you will certainly have a more exciting and enjoyable game.

Chapter 9 Progress in Performance

To become a better player you must play competitive games. Match play against weaker opponents enables you to consolidate and develop the work you have done in practice. Strong opponents provide you with a test of that work. If you want to know how you are progressing you must assess your performance after the match; then you can decide whether or not you are lacking in any aspect of the game. To do this you must also assess your opponent's performance, for it is what you do against each other that results in the game from which you can judge your performance. Hence you need information about your opponent as well as yourself. It makes sense, doesn't it? If you know how he plays and what you need to defeat him, then you can do something about improving your chances of winning next time you play him.

In general, most players tend to assess the game, so there is nothing new about it. Unfortunately, often it is not done very well, for an assessment of the game usually depends on how much you can remember about the game. Some players are very good at reflecting on the game and remembering lots of details about what went on in the game. Most players are not very good at this and only remember the highlights and superficial details, so they do not really obtain a good picture of what actually happened. Even if you have a very good memory and can recall the game in detail, you must still know what questions to ask about your performance and your opponent's performance in order to extract useful information from the game. It must be 'useful', for it must be an aid to improve your performance.

Thus we arrive at the following conclusion: to assess your performance in the game you require an accurate record of the game from which to obtain information about your respective performance. The problem is, quite simply, how to do this? There are several methods available. The ideal method would be to film the game using videotape linked directly with a computer programmed to give instant analysis and advice. This is a very real possibility in the future with the development of the professional game and the national prestige at stake in international team events; but, at present, it is beyond the interest and the means of most of us. What is needed is some simple, effective method of recording which could be followed up by a questionnaire to extract sufficient information to help you to improve your game and defeat the opponent. In this chapter, I shall describe such a simple system.

Badminton notation

This is a method of recording badminton using a system of symbols. Each stroke-move is recorded by a symbol. It is simple and logical, easy to learn and quite accurate.

The advantages of notation

It is a cheap and effective method of accurately recording a game. Each stroke-move is recorded as the game progresses. A complete and detailed record of a match is written down and can be studied immediately. This is a tremendous advantage compared with film, video tape or even sound recording. Even if it were possible to set up the equipment and meet the cost of such methods, it would still be necessary to record details on paper in order to examine and compare the situations and details of the game.

It would be interesting, from the historical point of view, to be able to read a notated record of some of the great players of the game: perhaps to study Hartono and compare him with Kops or Wong Peng Soon; see the stroke-moves used in certain situations, the effect of pressure, the reaction to vital stages of the match, the tactics used against different styles of player. It would certainly be useful information for the serious student of the game.

The purpose of notation

Basically the purpose is to gain information. There are many aspects of the game which are open to examination and analysis. Briefly, notation records a match and allows the following areas of a game to be recorded:

1. It records the detail in a game.
2. It shows clearly the patterns of play and the movement behaviour of a player during a match.
3. It shows the strengths and weaknesses of a player.
4. It attracts immediate attention to a weakness and shows clearly the type of situation which causes the weakness.
5. It shows the effect of motivation or lack of it on the choice of stroke-moves.
6. It emphasises fatigue periods during a match.
7. It shows the effect of pressure on the stroke-moves used.
8. It shows clearly the movement behaviour of a player in situations of stress during a match.

How can this information be used?

You can gain an accurate insight into and a sound knowledge of the opponent's game. With this knowledge and insight you can work out appropriate tactics and take calculated risks in set situations. You can examine your game, identify your weaknesses and any particular set habits you may be developing. Finally, for the coach, it is of obvious advantage. It draws attention to a recurring weakness. It directs the coach towards those aspects of the game that require his attention. He obtains accurate information which enables him to plan his work accordingly. Above all, it teaches you to look critically at the game; and if you can do that you will learn and understand more about the game.

The symbols They derive from the three basic moves. These are:

1. To hit the shuttle past the opponent to the rearcourt. The overhead clear or the underarm clear (lob) are used to hit the shuttle over his head and down the line to get past him to the rearcourt.
2. To hit the shuttle into the forecourt. Here the overhead drop-shot or the underarm block to the smash or net reply are used.
3. To hit the shuttle down so that it travels quickly to the midcourt. Here the smash and the variations on the smash are used to make the move.

The symbols below show the basic moves and their replies, with additional symbols used to show other important information.

Stroke-moves		*Replies*	*Additional information*	
sl	= serve low	n h lw	x	= cross-court
sh	= serve high	c d s	fh	= forehand
s	= smash	b l w	bh	= backhand
c	= clear	c d s	wk	= weak reply in a situation
d	= dropshot	n l h w	m	= miss shuttle completely
b	= block	n l w h	f	= fail to return shuttle in court
l	= lob	c d s	●	= in the net
w	= whip	s c d	○	= out of court
n	= net reply in forecourt	n l hw		
h	= hit down in forecourt	b l		

Recording

The recording sheet The recording sheet should contain the details of the match.

1. Name of tournament
2. Venue
3. Date
4. Event
5. Round
6. Names of players

Here are two methods of recording the play using this system of notation.

Method 1 The recording sheet contains vertical columns. Each column is divided into boxes to represent the court. Each box is divided in half across the width and along the length. The column reads from the top to the bottom and the symbols are placed in the box as if you were looking at the court from above. Thus one player is at the top end and the other at the bottom. Both players' courts are divided into a forehand and backhand side (see below, fig. 18).

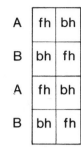

Fig. 18

Recording the stroke-moves

Each stroke is recorded as if you were sitting directly behind the player making the stroke-moves (see fig. 22).

Scoring

The score is shown on the left side of each column. The server's score is written first to ensure clarity in the sequence of stroke-moves in each rally (see fig. 22).

Recording a rally

Each rally commences with the serve shown by the symbol 'sl' or 'sh' designating a low or high serve.

Each rally is concluded by a double line. A game is concluded by a triple line.

Each box is written in sequence of AB AB . . .

When there is a change of serve, the serve commences in the box opposite the server's letter, A or B.

The final event refers to the ending of the rally and is always recorded. It takes place in the court of the player whose turn it is to hit the shuttle whether he does so or not. For example, if A smashes and B fails to return the shuttle into the court or misses it completely then that fact is recorded.

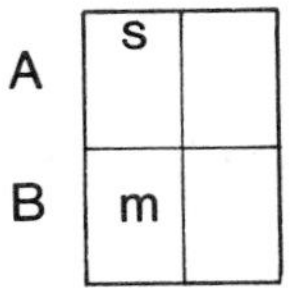

Fig. 19

A smashes and B misses it. The recording must show this for it draws attention to what B did or did not do in reply to the smash (see fig. 19).

This is most important for in any analysis it helps to know how each rally was won. In fig. 19, A won the rally not because he hit the smash, but because B missed it. If B continually misses the smash then we want to look at the defence of B or his previous move in the situation that A created. In fig. 20, A lost the rally because he smashed out over B's rearcourt. In fig. 21, A lost the rally because he hit the shuttle into the net. All this information is necessary in order to make accurate judgements about performance in the game.

The symbols for 'out of court' (○) and 'in the net' (●) are placed as shown in fig. 20 and fig. 21. The symbol '○' is placed next to the line in the box near to the part of the court into which it failed to land.

Fig. 20   Fig. 21

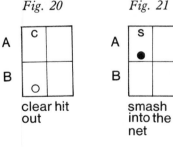

clear hit out

smash into the net

Learning to record

To record a game in detail is quite demanding and can be hard work. Practice in using the symbols and in concentrating for long periods is essential. Begin by recording a few details and gradually progress towards recording every detail. Here are some practical suggestions.

1. Position yourself behind the court opposite one corner. The length of the court then corresponds to the vertical column of the recording sheet. From this position it is easier to observe the game and to record.

2. Build up concentration slowly. Record only a few rallies at a time. Increase this to recording a game and finally a match.

3. Record only simple details at first. For example, record the symbol and don't worry about placing it accurately in the correct side of its box, i.e. forehand or backhand side. As you improve, place the symbol accurately, in the approximate position in the box relative to the court. Regular practice in using the symbols will improve your accuracy, speed and concentration.

Notation in operation

The example below shows a few rallies extracted from a recorded match. Player A versus player B.

Fig. 22

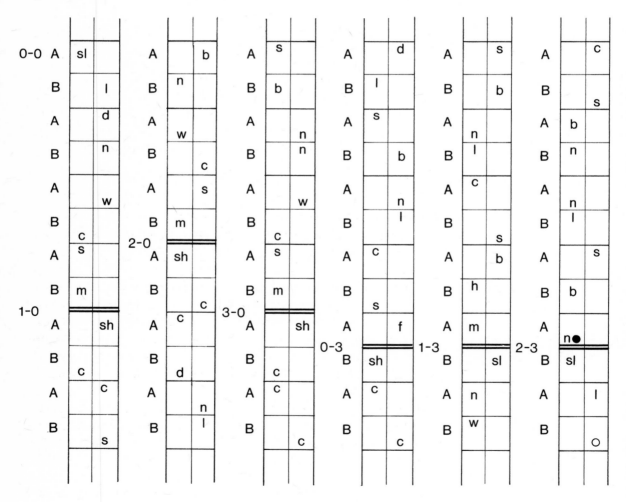

Description of play in the extract

Play begins in column 1 on the left of the sheet. Read the play from the top downwards.

Score: 1st game. Love all. Player A to serve.

0–0 Low serve
    Lob to the backhand rearcourt
    Drop to the forehand forecourt
    Net reply to the forecourt
    Whip x-court to backhand RC
    Weak clear to the forehand MC
    Smash to backhand MC
    Miss (fail to hit it). End of rally.

1–0 High serve to backhand RC
    Clear to backhand RC
    Clear to forehand RC
    Smash to backhand MC
    Block to backhand FC
    Net reply to forehand FC
    Whip to forehand RC
    Weak clear to backhand MC
    Smash to backhand MC
    Miss (fail to hit). End of rally.

2–0 Serve high to centre rearcourt.
    Continue and try to work out the remaining rallies yourself.

Method 2   This method uses the same symbols and is easier and quicker to use. It provides you immediately with an outline of the patterns of play and the form the game is taking. However, it does not provide you with as much visual information about the situations from which the stroke-moves are made. In Method 1 it is not necessary to use the x-court symbol (x), for the direction is clearly shown within the boxes representing the court. In Method 2 this is necessary.

    The direction of each stroke-move is assumed to be 'straight' unless shown by the x-court symbol. All stroke-moves are assumed to be forehands unless shown by the backhand symbol (bh).

    For example: xs   represents the x-court smash
                  bhc   represents the backhand clear

You may find the second method more desirable for the patterns of play become apparent as you record and so make subsequent analysis that much easier. This will become obvious as you study the method below.

The recording sheet

The recording sheet contains horizontal rows divided into boxes to show the sequence of stroke-moves used in a rally. Each box records the stroke-move used by each player. A rally reads along the row from left to right. The sequence of rallies is from top to bottom of the sheet (see below, fig. 23).

Score	A	B	A	B	A	B	A	B	A	B
0-0 A	sl	l	d	n	l	s	b●			
0-0 B		sl	l	c	d	n	l	c	dx	f

Fig. 23

The symbols '●' (in the net) and '○' (out of court) apply as in Method 1, except that the symbol '○' is placed in the box in which the next stroke-move would be made (see fig. 24 below).

Score	A	B	A	B	A	B
0-0 A	s	c	s●			
0-0 B		s	l	c	○	

Fig. 24

Recording a rally

You simply record the stroke-move played by players A or B in sequence in the correct box in the row. The score is written before the player's letter (A or B) to show the score before the rally commences. When the rally ends the score is written in the row below, next to the server's letter. Then you continue to record the play.

When there is a change of service remember to start recording in the box under the player who serves (see fig. 23 above).

Notation in operation

The rallies below are identical to the previous example, fig. 22.

Score	A	B	A	B	A	B	A	B	A	B	A	B	A	B	A
0-0 A	sl	l	d	n	wx	c	s	m							
1-0 A	sh	c	c	s	bx	n	wx	c	sx	m					
2-0 A	sh	cx	c	dx	n	lx	s	bx	n	n	wx	c	s	m	
3-0 A	sh	c	cx	c	dx	l	sx	b	n	lx	c	sx	f		
0-3 B		sh	cx	c	s	bx	n	l	cx	s	bx	h	m		
1-3 B		sl	n	wx	c	sx	b	n	n	l	s	b	n●		
2-3 B		sl	lx	○											

Fig. 25

Even in these few rallies shown it is possible to discern similar patterns emerging. Study them and see if you can recognise them. If not then let us try to analyse the rallies and see what we find. We can begin by asking a few simple questions.

How did A win his rallies?

How did B lose his rallies?

What did B do to prevent A winning the rallies?

How did B win his rallies?

How did A lose his rallies?

Let's look at A first. What we will do, is write out the final moves of each rally that A won or lost and see if we can learn anything from that.

Analysis sheet

Player	Score preceding rally / Result of rally		Final event	Preceding events				
A	0-0	won	B missed	A smash	B weak clear	A whip	B net	A drop
A	1-0	won	B missed	A smash	B weak clear	A whip	B net	A block
A	2-0	won	B missed	A smash	B weak clear	A whip	B net	A block
A	3-0	lost	A failed to return	B smash	A clear	B lift	A net	B block
A	1-3	lost	A hit in net	B block	A smash	B lift	A net	B net
A	2-3	lost	out	A lob	B serve low			

Fig. 26

If we trace the stroke-moves back from the final event, a distinct pattern begins to emerge. A won his rallies by hitting a smash which B did not return. But that doesn't tell us very much. Of far more interest is the fact that A created the situation to obtain a weak return from B, by bringing B into the forecourt to play a net rally. Once B played a net return to A's net stroke-move then A whipped the shuttle past B to the rearcourt, thus forcing a weak return.

By the fourth rally B had caught on and changed his tactics. Instead of playing a reply to the forecourt, B lifted to the rearcourt and forced A back to the rearcourt. In opening up the game, B prevented A from using the whip as a move from the forecourt to create a situation in which to make a scoring hit. At this stage of the game, A tended to lose the remaining rallies rather than B win them, as you can see in the analysis sheet.

Look again at the questions and you will find that we have answered them with this simple method of analysing.

What can A and B learn from this analysis? If we base our advice on what we have seen then it would seem, at this stage, that we are in a position to help B. It is clear that B's net play needs improving. Whatever he does is not sufficient to prevent A whipping the shuttle from the net to the rearcourt. It is also clear that B needs to do some work on his ability to travel and hit shuttles that get past him to the rearcourt. Or, failing that, he might send a weak clear because he tries to hit an attack clear, which he is not in a position to do successfully. It may be that he ought to use a defensive clear and hit the shuttle high and deep to the rearcourt and so give himself more time to make the move under such pressure. This stroke-move would also allow him more time to recover and perhaps be in a position to defend against the smash. At the present time, it would also appear that his defence is suspect, for he doesn't even reach the shuttle. The analysis shows patterns of play which clearly indicate possible reasons for the winning or losing of a rally. It should be apparent, that it is not sufficient to make any judgements about your performance on the basis of the final event in a rally, i.e. the winning hit or the mistake. What you want to know is how you arrived at the position to win or lose the rally.

We can now go a stage further and ask a few specific questions about the game. This takes the form of a questionnaire which can be applied to your game just as effectively as it can to your opponent's.

Questionnaire

1. Serving – the opening move
What situation does he create with the low serve, i.e. centre or sides?
What situation does he create with the high serve, i.e. rearcourt sides or centre; attack or defensive serve?
How does he recover after the serve, i.e. attack or defensive position in the midcourt?
What do you think would be a good reply to any serve in the situations he creates?

2. Receiving the serve
Where does he position himself to receive a serve?
What stroke-moves does he make in reply to the low serve and the high serve; from the forehand and backhand sides?

3. Rearcourt stroke-moves
What attitude does he adopt?
What moves does he make from a high position; at the sides and centre?
What move does he make from a low position?

How does he recover after making any stroke-move?

What is the function of his move?

What sort of reply do you think he expects to get from you?

What reply(ies) would be effective against him?

4. Midcourt stroke-moves

What attitude does he adopt?

What moves does he make from a high position, i.e. sides or centre, backhand and forehand side?

What moves does he make from a low position on the forehand and backhand side?

How does he recover after the different stroke-moves?

What is the function of his move?

What sort of reply does he expect from you?

What reply (ies) would be effective against him?

5. Forecourt stroke-moves

What attitude does he adopt?

What moves does he make above net level, just below net level, and near the ground?

How does he recover after a particular stroke-move?

What sort of reply does he expect and prepare for?

Does he cover all your possible replies?

What replies might be effective against him in this situation?

6. General questions

What is his favourite stroke-move, if any, in a particular situation?

What is his strongest stroke-move in a particular situation, in relation to your game?

What is his weakest stroke-move in a particular situation, in relation to your game?

Is there any particular pattern of stroke-moves he uses to create a situation which enhances his chances of making a scoring hit? In what situation does he make most of his scoring hits?

7. Deception

Does he use deception?

In what situations does he use deception?

What particular stroke-move does he use for deception?

How does he try to deceive you?

How does he recover after using deception?

What sort of replies do you think he expects?

8. Fitness

Does he travel quickly between situations?

Does he recover quickly after making a stroke-move?

Does he attack continually?

What is his state after a long hard rally:

a. If he wins it? b. If he loses it?

After a long rally can he:
  a. Play another long rally?
  b. Does he try for a scoring blow before he has created the right situation?
  c. Does he make errors in his stroke production?
How does fatigue affect his travelling?
  a. Speed or reaction time
  b. Ability to travel backwards
  c. Ability to travel forwards
  d. Ability to change direction quickly
  e. His recovery
Does his state of fitness affect his attitude at different phases of the game?

9.   Type of player What type of situation player is he: the sort that plays within a complete framework, incomplete or badly constructed framework?
How does he react under pressure?
Does he alter his game when he is losing or winning? If so, what does he do differently?

10.   Anything else you can think of?

Making use of the information gained about performance in the game

There are a number of different ways this information can be used to improve your performance and enable you to become more successful in competition. They are interrelated but we will discuss each separately.

1.   Profile of each opponent

Use the questionnaire to complete a profile on each opponent. This way it is possible to maintain a detailed record of all possible opponents and to obtain information when necessary. A study of the profile prior to the game will recall all the various aspects of the opponent's performance. It is simply a case of reminding yourself of the sort of situations you are likely to find yourself in. It gives you time to think prior to going on court. You might plan some tactics along the following lines.

What sort of moves does he make in various situations and what counter-moves can you make? Do his moves allow you to make use of them to create a situation in which to deliver a scoring hit? If so, write down the situation and the counter-moves you could make. Work out how the opponent might counter your move so you are ready to meet his counter.

The order is:
  ● his move – your replies
  ● using his move to make a possible counter move
  ● his possible counters
  ● your reply

With careful study it is not too difficult to develop a tactic for each possible pattern of stroke-moves that your opponent uses.

2. Practice

After analysing the game with respect to the performance of your opponent and yourself, you are now in a better position to design realistic and meaningful practices.

The questions you should now ask are:

What are your needs in the game?

How will you satisfy those needs?

Are they technical, tactical or both?

What weaknesses do you need to work on?

What strengths do you need to develop?

Write out a list of your technical and tactical needs and then design your practices. When you have done that you can get down to some hard beneficial work.

3. Mental rehearsal

The analysis of the game and the answers to the questionnaire will provide you with an adequate picture of the opponent's game. This is reinforced with the work you do in the tactical practices specifically designed to give you experience in the sort of situation you might meet against a particular opponent. Some players use this experience and insight into an opponent's game to rehearse mentally the possible contest as a final preparation before they actually play. Players have different ways of doing this all of which require a quiet period of concentration and reflection. The player uses his imagination to bring the contest to mind. He pictures himself serving, the opponent's reply and the subsequent rallies. Gradually the game takes shape as he 'sees' patterns of play emerging and he becomes familiar once again with that opponent. He need not have played his opponent previously to rehearse the contest in this way. It is possible to study and become familiar with another player's game through careful observation. Of course, it is of more advantage if you have played the opponent previously. Nevertheless, mental rehearsal does contribute to your state of readiness and your 'reading' of the game in actual play. It is worth considering as a method of preparation.

4. On planning and play

It is not intended that you do all this study and practice in order to go on court with preconceived plans which you put into operation regardless of the way the game develops. Neither are you expected, nor is it desirable, to theorise on court in the middle of a match. The whole purpose of this work is to free you from ignorance; to equip you fully to deal with any situation that arises; to enable you to create situations to your advantage; and finally to enable you to free yourself from conscious thought. You should be able to play with free use of the imagination, acting intuitively in the situations that arise in the game. You should be able to play without thought, free from any restrictions and handicaps within your performance. A knowledge of what your opponent does has been a useful guide to designing meaningful practices. So in practice you will have learned to contend with any situation where there might have been a weakness. Now you can go on court and concentrate on playing in your own way, not having to worry about how your opponent plays. You can leave him to worry about how you play.

This is one of the considerable benefits of the hard work that you do in preparation for match play. The more you study, think and prepare yourself mentally off the court, the less mental work you have to do on the court. The more physical work you do in training getting fit, the less you need that fitness in the game. The more time that you spend on technical and tactical practices, the easier it becomes to perform strokes and create situations in the contest. Your game eventually becomes more simplified in competition relative to how much work you put in developing it in practice and training. You do more work in preparation in order to do less work in competition. If you have done the work you should be able to step on the court fully confident that you are prepared. Once the game begins you should become absorbed in the present moment, without thought for the past or for the future, and become totally immersed in the battle. You should focus all your attention and direct all your energy towards your opponent. And play with one target only. To win!

3 1543 50002 1979

796.345
D748w

DATE DUE

796.345
D748w

Downey
Winning
badminton
singles

DATE

NO 21 86

Cressman Library
Cedar Crest College
Allentown, Pa. 18104

DEMCO